Arabian Love Poems

قصائدُ حُبّ عربيّة

Nizar Kabbani

نزار قباني

To Nick, thank you
for being a friend.
Sending you unconditional
"I will chop my arm off for you"
Arab Love - Happy Birthday

A Three Continents Book

Arabian Love Poems

Nizar Kabbani

Full Arabic and English Texts

Translated by
Bassam K. Frangieh
and Clementina R. Brown

LYNNE
RIENNER
PUBLISHERS

BOULDER
LONDON

Published in the United States of America in 1999 by
Lynne Rienner Publishers, Inc.
1800 30th Street, Boulder, Colorado 80301

and in the United Kingdom by
Lynne Rienner Publishers, Inc.
3 Henrietta Street, Covent Garden, London WC2E 8LU

Library of Congress Cataloging-in-Publication Data
Qabbānī, Nizār.
    [Poems. English & Arabic. Selections]
    Arabian love poems / Nizar Kabbani = Qaṣā'id ḥubb 'Arabīyah /
Nizār Qabbānī.—Rev. ed.
        p.   cm.
    English and Arabic.
    Translated by Bassam K. Frangieh and Clementina R. Brown, with an
introduction by Bassam K. Frangieh.
    Includes bibliographical references (p.   ) and index.
    ISBN 978-0-89410-881-5 (pb : alk. paper)
    1. Qabbānī, Nizār.—Translations into English. 2. Qabbānī, Nizār.—
Translations into English. I. Frangieh, Bassam K. II. Brown,
Clementina R. III. Title. IV. Title: Qaṣā'id ḥubb 'Arabīyah.
PJ7858.A2A24   1998
892.71'6—dc21   98-42796
                                                             CIP

British Cataloguing in Publication Data
A Cataloguing in Publication record for this book
is available from the British Library.

Printed and bound in the United States of America

12 11 10

Contents

⚊ From *One Hundred Love Letters* ⚊

Other Poems

Preface

~

ON APRIL 30, 1998, NIZAR KABBANI, THE MOST POPULAR ARAB poet of the twentieth century, died at age 75 in London. The battle for his life, waged against complications resulting from several heart attacks, lasted four months. Syrian president Hafez Al-Assad, who had just two months earlier decided to name a major street after Kabbani in Abu Roummana, the most prestigious district in Damascus, dispatched his own plane to carry Kabbani's body back to the city of his birth. Kabbani had asked in his will to be buried in his native land: "I want my body to be transported after my death to Damascus to be buried there with my people." Kabbani continued in his will, "Damascus is the womb that taught me poetry, creativity and the alphabet of Jasmine. I want to return home like the bird returns home and like the baby returns to his mother's bosom."

Kabbani, a devoted and committed Arab nationalist, was "hailed across Syria as a national hero," wrote the *New York Times* on the day following his death.[1] Al-Assad sent a member of his cabinet to extend his personal condolences to the family, and Kabbani's coffin was draped with the Syrian flag in one of the largest funeral services in the country's history. On the afternoon of a torrid May 4, a massive number of people crammed into the street in front of Badr Mosque, where the poet's funeral took place. The newspaper *Ash-Sharq Al-Awsat* estimated that more than ten thousand people walked in the three-hour funeral procession to Bab al-Shaghour, where the poet was laid to rest next to his father, mother, sister, and son.[2] The mourners included the minister of defense, the governor of Damascus, other high-level government officials, Syrian Ba'thist leaders, Arab writers, members of influential organizations, unionists, artists, and journalists. Traditionally, Syrian women have not participated in such large public processions. Still, a large number of women attended the funeral—women who had been deeply touched over the years by Kabbani's verses, which spoke directly to them, about them, and for them.

Outside of his native Syria, the poet was mourned by millions of Arabs all over the world. Major newspapers reported on the loss: The *London Times* described Kabbani as "the Arab World's greatest love poet in modern times,"[3] while the *Washington Post* called him "the master of the love verse."[4] The *New York Times* obituary quoted a Syrian poet who said that Kabbani has been "as necessary to our lives as air."[5] Most radio and television stations in the Arab world interrupted their regular programs to announce the sad news of Kabbani's death. Virtually every Arabic-language newspaper carried extensive front-page coverage of his death, with additional articles on his life and achievements. For weeks, not a day passed without a major commentary in the Arabic press detailing his significance to Arab society.

Leading Arab intellectuals expressed great sorrow at the vacuum Kabbani left in Arabic poetry and culture. Poet Abdul Wahab Al-Bayati, a pioneer in the free-verse movement that swept the Arab world in the 1950s, said: "The poetry of Nizar Kabbani has been a mirror of an entire age and served as a history for Arab aspirations and hopes that were crushed after the June 1967 Arab defeat. He stood alone in his poetic style and diction with a unique texture. The many poets who tried to imitate him have all failed."[6] Lebanese critic and professor Muhammed Najm, who recently edited a two-volume set of literary criticism in honor of Kabbani's work, reflected that "no Arab poet has surpassed Kabbani in either originality or innovation. Once he fully mastered classical Arabic poetry, he moved on to modern Western literature, then produced profound poems with extreme simplicity."[7]

Novelist Tayeb Salih commented that "an Arab World without Nizar Kabbani is very difficult to imagine. Kabbani devoted his life to the Arab World for fifty years, engaging himself in all social situations, in all victories and defeats, in our sadness and joy, and he stood at the heart of all Arab events, always defying and provoking, encouraging and satirizing. Events got their full meanings only when he described them. Victories were not considered victories until Kabbani said that they were victories, and the dimensions of defeats were not clearly understood until Kabbani pointed them out." It is as if, Salih added in his *Ash-Sharq Al-Awsat* piece, "lovers did not learn the meaning of love until they read the poetry of Nizar Kabbani."[8]

To say that Kabbani was the most popular and famous of contemporary Arab poets is not to claim that he was the most skilled. Others far surpassed him in vision and sophistication; but their complex verses, charged with metaphysics and metaphor, were accessible only to the intellectuals and the highly educated. Kabbani's verses addressed the crises facing the people: the realities of high unemployment, the challenge of earning enough to bring home bread and rice to one's family, the interrogations and investigations made by the police and secret service against innocent citizens, the series of dictators and their political mafias in the years since independence. Kabbani wrote in a language that was close to the language spoken in the home and in the street. He used images close to the heart, with a mystical, penetrating musicality that altered Arab political consciousness. As a result, his poems were read in cafés, in parks, in office buildings, and on street corners. His was a strong voice for the millions of oppressed Arabs who would not talk for fear of political or social persecution. He will always be remembered as the poet who was more politically effective than any modern Arab political party. His poetry was described as "more powerful than all the Arab regimes put together."[9]

Readers will also surely miss Kabbani's prose. He was a writer sought by the most influential newspapers and magazines in the Arab world, and his columns gained readers for any paper lucky enough to publish them. People anxiously awaited his boldly provocative criticisms of the most recent political developments in the Middle East. He was always on top of current events. Always rebellious. Always dissatisfied. Always loud and confrontational. The masses saw in his words a compass amid the chaos of Arab reality and its unclear future direction. Kabbani was a mainstream leader who called for resistance and radicalism in the shadow of a failed Middle East peace process and a stagnant Arab culture, refusing to accept either. Along with a number of other nationalist writers, he opposed normalization with Israel. He openly battled Naguib Mahfouz, the Egyptian Nobel Prize winner for literature, who supported normalization.

Kabbani was unique: Although he attacked rulers, he was never thrown in jail. Although his books were banned in some Arab countries, he remained the world's best-selling Arab poet. Although he addressed his verses to the poor and the oppressed, he never associated with them, unlike other poets such as Al-Bayati, who spent time in cafés and public places, drinking coffee with ordinary people, listening to their problems, and offering advice. Kabbani never dropped a bourgeois mentality and an elitist attitude.

(This last comment is not intended as criticism. The Syrian bourgeois class during the French mandate and in the 1940s, when Kabbani was in his formative years, was divided for the most part into two groups. The first group "sold out," serving as local agents for the imperialists, imitating the French, visiting casinos, dancing the tango, and spending their summers in Paris. The second group, which included the Kabbani family, was the "nationalist" bourgeois: They played a major role in provoking the people to struggle against the French mandate and in developing a national political consciousness; they also served as arms brokers both to finance the nationalist movement and to supply the members of the resistance with weapons for fighting against the French occupation. Kabbani's father was one of the national bourgeois who helped to finance and organize the Syrian National Movement.)

There is no Arab poet of equal caliber to Kabbani on the near horizon. He remains a powerful psychological outlet for millions who express their misery and pain through his verses. Those verses have been a necessity of life to many Arabs, from Morocco to the Gulf. Thus, in lamenting his death, Sulhi Al-Wadi wrote: "Kabbani is like water, bread, and the sun in every Arab heart and house. In his poetry the harmony of the heart, and in his blood the melody of love. His body has departed, but his soul is hovering over the Damascus to which he bid farewell with jasmine to be received with laurels. . . . Good-bye Nizar."[10]

* * *

Lynne Rienner called me in Cairo in May 1998 to express her interest in publishing a new edition of Nizar Kabbani's *Arabian Love Poems*, which I had translated with Clementina Brown in 1993. That call came at a time when I was both saddened by the poet's recent death and disappointed at the unavailability of the love poems, the Arabic text of which Kabbani had written in his own hand.

In the weeks following the poet's death, I read a daily deluge of obituaries and articles on his life and achievements. The more I read, the more I realized that no gesture of appreciation could equal ensuring the availability of his poetry. This new, revised edition of *Arabian Love Poems*, particularly meaningful so soon after Kabbani's death, is offered as a sincere appreciation of the elegance of Arabic poetry, and as a way to keep Kabbani's legacy alive in the English-speaking world.

Bassam K. Frangieh

NOTES

1. *New York Times*, May 1, 1998.
2. *Ash-Sharq Al-Awsat*, May 5, 1998.
3. *London Times*, May 14, 1998.
4. *Washington Post*, May 1, 1998.
5. *New York Times*, May 1, 1998.
6. *Ash-Sharq Al-Awsat*, May 1, 1998.
7. Ibid.
8. Ibid.
9. *Lebanese Daily Star*, May 5, 1998.
10. *Tishreen*, May 2, 1998.

Introduction

Bassam K. Frangieh

—

NIZAR KABBANI, THE MOST INFLUENTIAL AND BEST-KNOWN Arab poet in modern times, penetrated and captured the hearts and souls of millions of Arabs. During a career that produced fifty volumes of poetry, Kabbani became the Arab world's greatest love poet. He was a champion of women's rights, urging women to take control of their lives, bodies, and destinies. A proponent of women's liberation, he initiated a change in attitudes about sexuality, erotic freedom, and the right of women to celebrate ecstasy.[1] He asserted that freedom of the body was a path to freedom of the spirit for everyone, thereby helping the new generation to erase the guilt, fear, and embarrassment that had been associated with sex.[2] He also strived to change the repressive relationship between the two sexes to one of openness.

Kabbani was born in Damascus, Syria, on March 21, 1923, to a traditional well-to-do family. He was the second of six children—two girls and four boys. During his youth, the resistance movement against the French mandate was mobilizing the population, and the modern nation of Syria was in the process of being born. Along with the other merchants and professionals, his father, Tawfiq Kabbani, a respected national figure, helped finance the national movement and was one of its leaders. The spacious Kabbani house, located in Al-Shaghur, the most conservative section of the city, was used for secret resistance meetings, and the child Nizar would sit in the huge courtyard near fountains and flowers listening to political leaders speak out against the French occupation.

There were calls for revolution and freedom, and plans for strikes and demonstrations were often completed in the Kabbani home. Early one morning when Nizar was ten, French soldiers entered the house and arrested his father, imprisoning him for a time in the Syrian desert outside Palmyra. The example set by his father, who was willing to sacrifice for political and social freedom, laid the foundation for Kabbani's later work and influenced his poetic development.

Kabbani may also have been influenced by his father's uncle, Abu Khalil al-Kabbani, who was an unusual and gifted nineteenth-century

Syrian figure. Abu Khalil was a well-known author, composer, singer, dancer, actor, and poet who was strongly influenced by Western theater. He translated Moliere into Arabic and established the first theater company in Syria. He long dreamed of creating a "Broadway district" in the city of Damascus.

Because women were not allowed to act in the Syrian theater during Abu Khalil's time, he gave female roles to young men with high-pitched voices. This female impersonation enraged the sheikhs and religious figures in Damascus, and they sent a delegation to the capital of the Ottoman Empire to complain to the caliph. A decree was issued to close Abu Khalil's theater, the only avant-garde theater in the Middle East at that time. Forced into exile, Abu Khalil went to Egypt, where he soon began to contribute to the establishment of the Egyptian theater at the end of the century.

Nizar Kabbani attended primary and secondary school at the National College of Science, located in the heart of old Damascus. This college, established for the Damascene bourgeois, combined in its curriculum Arabic and French languages and cultures, in contrast to the missionary schools, where only French language and culture were emphasized. The faculty of the National College included leading intellectuals, writers, and poets, and Kabbani was fortunate to have been taught by the gifted poet Khalil Mardam.

Kabbani completed secondary school and then earned his bachelor's degree in law from Damascus University. Although it was his major, he did not like law, preferring instead to jot down love poems in the margins of his notebooks during classroom lectures.

According to the poet, he came from a family that falls in love easily: "Love was born in my family as natural as sweetness is born in apples." For generations, men in the Kabbani family were known for falling in love with the first pair of beautiful eyes they saw. Wissal Kabbani, one of the poet's sisters, was herself a martyr to love. Kabbani was fifteen when Wissal committed suicide, "simply and poetically," because she couldn't marry the man she loved. The image of his sister dying for the sake of love lived on in his memory, and he often thought of her "angelic face and her beautiful smile" while she was dying.[3]

Nizar Kabbani believed that his sister's suicide may have been one of the factors that led him to devote himself to love poetry. He wrote, "The death of my sister, the martyr, broke something inside me and left on the surface of the lake of my childhood more than one ripple and more than one question mark."[4]

He wrote his first poem in 1939, at age sixteen, and in 1944 published his first collection of love poems, *Qalat li al-Samra'* (The Brunette Said to Me). In this collection, the twenty-one-year-old poet described how he had discovered the world of women and the world of love. Full of sexual images, the work became available during a time when love and sex were forbidden topics in Arab society, especially among the youth, and it sold out within a month. Verses in the collection spread like wildfire, and one poem, "Your Breast," catapulted Kabbani to fame. In it, the poet talks to a brunette:

Unlock the treasury!
Lay bare your burning breasts
Don't smother your imprisoned fire.
Your breasts are the two most beautiful paintings,
Two balls of silk spun by the generous morning,
So come close to me my little cat
Let yourself free,
Come close,
Think of the fate of your breasts
With the turn of the seasons.
Don't panic,
Foolish is she who hides her breasts
And lets her youth pass without being kissed.
I pulled her body to me
She neither resisted nor spoke,
Intoxicated she swayed against me
And offered her quivering breasts
Saying in drunken passion
"I cannot resist touching fire."[5]

Students gathered together to recite this poem, copying lines in their schoolbooks, and verses appeared on every schoolroom blackboard in Damascus. In appreciation of his young fans, Kabbani noted, "Throughout my poetic history, students have been my troops, my voice, and my passport to the world."[6]

The collection—twenty-eight poems written in a new style, simple, direct, and honest—appeared toward the end of World War II, when Damascene society was undergoing a transformation. Previously, literary life had been isolated from the people and molded by rigid rules and traditional themes. During the war years, however, an intergenerational struggle began, which Kabbani embodied. Expressing the needs of the new generation for openness and social freedom, he broke the entrenched walls of silence about love and sex and established a contemporary, liberated love poetry. The younger generation also responded enthusiastically to the poet's style, in which classical Arabic was linked with colloquial words. Kabbani often used pure Damascene idioms in his verses. His work was read by young men and women in their bedrooms and in the streets. They felt that this poet was speaking their language and using a vocabulary of yearning, excitement, love, lust, and rebellion—a true expression of their lives.[7] Predictably, the poet was attacked by conservatives in Syria and other Arab states who had a vested interest in traditional lifestyles.

Harshly criticized by the clergy and religious leaders as had been his uncle earlier in the century, Kabbani also was attacked by the media. Among his most bitter critics was Sheikh Ali Tantawi, who published a series of caustic articles in *Al-Risala Journal*. Sheikh Tantawi wrote:

> A year ago in Damascus a little book was published with a glossy, smooth cover like the fancy paper which is used to wrap chocolate at weddings. The book is tied with a red ribbon like the one the French used at the beginning of their occupation of Damascus to girdle the hips of some women. This book is supposed to be poetry but the verses are of equal length only if you measure them with a ruler. The collection contains a description of a shameless whore and every festering and sinful thing. It is a realistic description but without imagination because the author is not an imaginative man. Rather he is a spoiled school boy, rich and dear to his parents.[8]

A year after the controversial collection was published, Kabbani joined the Syrian diplomatic corps, subsequently serving in Cairo, Ankara, London, Madrid, Beijing, and Beirut. This experience played an important role in his life and his art, for his ever more complex and allusive style seems to reflect his long immersion in foreign cultures.[9] Nonetheless, he continued to publish poems in which he described his deepening feelings about women and his sympathies for their deprivations and unequal treatment.

In 1948, he published his second collection, *Tufulat Nahd* (Young Breast), another important achievement. The relative openness of Cairo, his first post, had further liberated the artist in him and refined his poetic language, introducing sensuous images within a complex aesthetic framework and symbolic expressions. In his collection *Qasa'id* (Poems), published in 1956, Kabbani further explored the inner world of women and established new trends in feelings and thought. Here, for the first time, he expressed himself in the first-person feminine. This is an important aspect of his poetry, through which the reader experiences the hidden world of women and hears their bitter words against men and society. In a sense, he was doing what his artistic uncle had done—using male voices to speak for the generations of silenced women.

Kabbani said it better in the introduction to his collection *Yawmiyyat Imra'a La-Mubaliya* (Diary of an Indifferent Woman), 1968, where he elaborated further on the societal pressures on Arab women: "This is the book of every woman . . . sentenced and executed before she could open her mouth. The East needs a man like me to put on the clothes of a woman and to borrow her bracelets and eyelashes in order to write about her. Is it not an irony that I cry out with a woman's voice while women cannot speak up on their own?"[10]

From the very beginning of his poetic career, Kabbani held Arab men and the society they dominated responsible for the wrongs done to women. He early understood the problems of women, and his position on the issue of women's rights remained unchanged. His poetry, early and late, with its social and aesthetic dimensions, made a difference. Kabbani, allying himself through his art with liberal forces at work in the Arab world, courageously produced vivid verses that created an atmosphere encouraging women to abandon the veil, to choose their marriage partners, and to gain a modest level of independence.

In the spring of 1966, Kabbani left the diplomatic service to devote himself entirely to his poetry. He remained in Beirut, his last post, and founded the publishing house Manshurat Nizar Kabbani to produce his works. Kabbani wrote: "When I sat behind the desk and lit the first cigarette in my Beirut office, I felt like a king with real authority."[11] The concept of love that Kabbani developed in his 1966 publication "Painting with Words" was one result of his twenty years of emotional, social, and poetic experience outside of Syria.

In his 1972 collection, *Ash'ar Kharija 'ala al-Qanun* (Poems Outside the Law), the reader finds symbolism intermixed with romanticism. It is a sharp and sensitive collection in which each poem changes into a symbol. The beautiful poem "Tanwi'at Musiqiyah 'an Imra'ah Mutajarridah"

(Musical Variations of a Naked Woman), for example, is a creative and innovative work depicting the feelings of a poet before two naked breasts. His feelings expand to include visions and images transferring the movements of the breasts into voices, smells, tastes, flames, and colors.[12] The poem is an artistic mixture of images, thoughts, and feelings, rich in details:

Two beautiful roosters
Crow on your chest
And sleep.
I remained sleepless.
The hand-embroidered sheet
Was covered with birds,
Roses and palm trees.

The fields of Ceylon,
The forests of spices,
And the coconuts
Call me,
Keeping me from sleep.
My nerves are pieces of straw,
My face a newspaper clipping.
I am not a killer,
But the jumping shark
In the gulf of your wild breasts
Seduced me into committing a crime.

Your half-open red gown
Revealing two firm breasts
Sliced my wound open.
I dreamt of you in your bath,
The iridescent bubbles
Floated by the chandelier, flicked my skin,
Broke me on the ground into pieces.

Your breasts were two baby lambs
Nuzzling on the grass of my chest,

Cashmere fleeced my face, my shirt.
I, shattered, glittered on the floor like beads . . .
Drinking coffee,
And your wet gown
Roused me,
Millions of gifts you offered.

Your breasts were two unbridled horses
Drinking water from the bottom of mirrors. . . .[13]

Kabbani rejected the silencing of love, just as he opposed societal values based on repression. Many of his verses sought to incite women to liberate themselves from constricting society.[14]

Love me and say it out loud,
I refuse that you love me mutely[15]

There is no poem by Kabbani that is free of a female presence, and there is nothing about women that Kabbani could not transform as an inspiration for his verse.

I become ugly when I don't love
And I become ugly when I don't write[16]

The supreme importance of women to Kabbani is indicated in the following verse, which depicts women as a source of protection, salvation, and supernatural power in the face of death:

Nothing protects us from death
Except woman and writing[17]

The poet paid a great deal of attention to the emotional lives of women and was fond of the "little things" that shape how they think and feel. In his poem "Shu'un Saghirah" (Little Things), he speaks in a woman's voice to reveal the way she feels when she is in love, describing the details and inner world that fill her life and enrich her imagination, and conveying her passion, warmth, and innocence:

Little things
Which mean the world to me
Pass by you
Without making an impression.
From these things
I build palaces,
Live on them for months
And spin many tales from them,
One thousand skies,
And one thousand islands,
But these little things
Mean nothing to you.

. . . .

When the telephone rings in our house
I run to it
With the joy of a small child,
I embrace the emotionless machine
And squeeze
Its cold wires
And I wait
For your warm, full voice to come to me
Like the music of falling stars
And the sound of tumbling jewels.
I cry
Because you have thought of me
And have called me
From the invisible world.

. . . .

When I return to my room in the evening
And take off my dress,
I feel your hands
Mercifully wrapping around my arms.
Although you are not in my room
I worship
The place where your warm hands
Held the sleeve of my blue dress
And cry.[18]

Kabbani played an important role in bringing poetic language closer to the language used in everyday life. Poet Salma Jayyusi argues that Kabbani did more than any other contemporary Arab poet to unite the language of poetry with contemporary language, both written and vernacular. In much of his erotic and sociopolitical verse he managed to approximate the rhythms of common speech. His poetry produces an instant effect on the audience. His contemporary voice is heard not only in the use of the single word, but also, and this is most important, in his style, his word arrangement, and the very spirit of the language.[19]

Leading critic Ihsan Abbas has argued that, if not for Nizar Kabbani and some of the poetry of Salah Abdul Sabour, love would not have taken the form of an independent poetic theme in the Arab world. Before these two poets, love had been mixed and blended with other themes. Kabbani gave the theme of love distinct dimensions that guaranteed its independent existence, and as a result, he was named the poet of love. Kabbani made love one part of an equation between two great powers: women and poetry.[20]

Kabbani also addressed problems facing women from a psychological or sociological point of view. The reaction of a woman to an unfaithful husband is examined in "Risalah Min Sayyidah Haqidah" (Letter from an Angry Woman). The problem of a pregnant woman whose lover turns his back on her is the subject of "Hubla" (Pregnant). How a woman might express her sexual hunger when the man close to her does not satisfy her is the theme of "Aw'iyat al-Sadid" (Vessels of Pus). And how this same woman then ceases from making love to men and begins to make love with women is the subject of "Al-Qasidah al-Shirirah" (The Evil Poem).[21]

Kabbani's poetry was not inspired by a single love or a single woman; it was the product of multiple relationships and much experience. His love had a universal tone and universal dimensions—a love for the entire world. He felt that he was part of the land, society, culture, and history, and that each word a poet puts on paper carries within it an entire humanity. "Woman for me is a continent that I travelled to, but she is certainly not the entire world. Love for me embraces the entire universe. It exists in the soil and water and in the night; in the wounds of fighters and in the eyes of children; in the revolutions of students and in the furor of angry men. Woman is a seaport among many seaports that provided me with bread, water, silk, and incense, but the rest of the ports continue calling to my ship.[22]

9

Kabbani saw in women a revolution and a means of liberation for both men and women. He linked women's rights with the war for social liberation in the Arab world, maintaining: "Unless we stop considering women as sex objects, there will be no liberation. Sexual repression is the biggest problem in the Arab World." He called for an end to the game of love behind closed doors: "I have moved my bed to the open air and I have written my love poems on trees in public parks . . . to put an end to secretive and marshal laws imposed on the body of the Arab woman and make love legitimate."[23] "People who are possessed with sex, he wrote, "cannot write, think, or undertake any civilized achievement."[24] Thus, he was convinced that sexual repression is one reason behind the economic backwardness of the Arab world, and that any revolution concerned solely with an individual's thoughts and not with his or her body is only half a revolution.

* * *

Kabbani believed that, ideally, art should be able to lift the veil from tragedy without seeking solutions. He touched upon his subject with the tenderness and delicacy of a butterfly, like a painter using his brush.[25] His skillful and hidden techniques require careful study.

Poetic language is the real key to Kabbani's work and was his most important achievement. "I departed from the dictionary and dealt with vocabulary that everyone used. I included words that are hot, fresh, and mixed with the flesh of human beings and the incidents in their daily lives." As he saw it, his task as a poet was to take poetry from the lips of individuals and return it to them. His words were always warm and directed to innocent, simple people, to those who "could not find clothes to wear so they wore a poem."[26] He portrayed the reality of his audience.

Kabbani also was an indisputable master of poetry readings. His readings were exceptional cultural events, and millions of Arabs gathered to listen to him in person, on television, or on the radio, affirming the importance of poetry in the lives of Arabs and in the molding of their consciousness. In Sudan, ten thousand people attended one of his open-air readings. During the Arab League's 1980 poetry festival in Tunis, he read his powerful poem "Ana Ya Sadiqati Mut'abun Bi'urubati" (My Friend, I Am Tired of My Arabism), which was broadcast on Tunisian National Television; it is said that the broadcast was watched by everyone in the country who had access to a television, and by the next day the poem had spread throughout the Middle East, where its verses can be found to this day framed on walls in homes.

More than those of any other contemporary Arab poet, Kabbani's poems have been set to music and recorded. Since popular music in the Arab world has a massive audience, these recordings have broadened Kabbani's appeal even further, capturing the hearts of millions of listeners and flowing from many lips. His verses serve as a bridge between popular music and modern poetry, and they have enriched popular Arabic music with poetic rhythms and nuances.

* * *

Although Kabbani mixed romanticism and symbolism with realism, his work is difficult to classify into one school or movement of poetic thought. He himself was well aware of this fact. In his 1990 volume *Hal Tasma'in Sahil Ahzani?* (Do You Hear the Neigh of My Sadness?), for example, he wrote: "Don't bother to classify me. I'm a poet outside classification, description and specifications. I'm not a traditionalist, a modernist, classicist, neoclassicist, romantic, nor a futurist, an impressionist, or surrealist. I'm a mixture that no laboratory can analyze. I'm a mixture of freedom. This is the word that I have been seeking for fifty years and I only found it this moment."[27]

* * *

It was in 1954 that Kabbani added another taboo to his poetry: politics. In that year he published "Khubz wa Hashish wa Qamar" (Bread, Hashish, and Moon), in which he harshly criticized the mistakes of the Arabs, attacking all Arab leaders in his demand for radical change. More than a decade later, after the Arab defeat in the Six Day War, he announced his commitment to political poetry:

O my sad homeland
You have changed me
In a single moment
From the poet writing of love and longing
To a poet writing with a knife[28]

"Woman has been my beloved for fifty years and still is," he wrote, "but I added to her a second wife; her name is Homeland."[29]

Kabbani's growing commitment to political poetry was not a surprise. The first poem he wrote had a nationalist theme, and he kept touching on other political and social themes.[30] His love and compassion for his country and his longing for his land were always strong, reflecting his family's deep roots in the national and social struggles in the Arab world. Traveling in Andalusia, he was swept by a storm of yearning for his homeland:

In the narrow streets of Cordova
I reached into my pockets more than once
To pull out the keys
To our house in Damascus[31]

In 1956, he wrote "The Story of Rachel Schwartzenberg," in which he summarized in poetic verses the story of the Zionist movement and the miserable situation of Palestinians living and struggling in the diaspora. Also in 1956, during the aggression of Britain, France, and Israel against Egypt, he wrote "Letter from a Soldier on the Suez Front," denouncing the attackers and depicting the heroism of the Egyptians as they defended their land. In 1961 he wrote "Jamila Buhayred," in which he described that woman's bravery and her prominent role in the Algerian struggle against the French.[32]

"Bread, Hashish, and Moon" (1954), however, was perhaps his most famous sociopolitical poem. In it he shook the foundations of Arab society by revealing a collapsing social system and calling for immediate change. The poet described in clear words the miserable situation of the masses who live in poverty, superstition, and backwardness:

When the moon is born in the east,
The white roofs sleep
Beneath the heaps of light,
People leave their shops and depart in groups
To meet the moon,
Carrying their bread and songs to the mountaintop,
And their drugs,
Where they buy and sell fantasies
And images,

And die if the moon comes to life.
What does that luminous disc
Do to my land,
To the land of the prophets,
To the land of the simple,
The chewers of tobacco and dealers of narcotics,
What does the moon do to us,
That we lose our pride
And live only to beg from heaven?
What does heaven have
For the lazy and the weak? . . .
They spread out their fine and elegant carpets
And console themselves with an opium
Called destiny and fate
In this land, the land of the simple.[33]

After the poem was published, the Syrian parliament met to discuss its implications, and some members of parliament demanded that its author be expelled from the Syrian foreign service.

The poem "Hawamish 'ala Daftar al-Naksah" (Marginal Notes on the Book of Defeat), which Kabbani wrote immediately after the 1967 Arab defeat, contained harsh criticism for the political, psychological, and strategic mistakes of the Arabs. This poem resulted in pitting both the right and the left against him because he attacked all Arab leaders without exception, calling for democracy, freedom, and justice:

It is not surprising that we have lost the war.
For we fought it
With all the East's rhetorical talents
And empty heroism.
. . . .
The secret of our tragedy:
Our cries are more powerful than our voices,
Our swords taller than our men.
. . . .
Our skins are numbed,
Our souls bankrupt,
Our days wasted in witchcraft, chess and sleep.
. . . .

O Sultan, O my lord,
Because I came close to your deaf walls,
Trying to reveal my sadness and my misfortune,
I was beaten with shoes.
Your soldiers forced me to eat out of my shoes.
O Sultan, O my lord,
You have lost the war twice
Because half of us has no tongue—
What value are people with no voice?[34]

The poem found a large audience among the many Arabs who read in it what they had wanted to say but were not able to put into words.

As happens to many artists of courage and vision, Kabbani paid a high price for writing political poetry. At one time or another, most of the Arab regimes have censored his books. In Egypt, after the publication of "Marginal Notes on the Book of Defeat," all of Kabbani's poetry, including his verses set to music, was banned; he was not allowed to enter the country, and there were calls for a trial. Eventually, however, after a personal appeal to Egyptian president Gamal Abdul Naser, Kabbani was given permission to travel in Egypt and his music and poetry were available again.

Kabbani's message is clear and consistent: the political and social structures in the Arab world must change to better represent the people. He vowed publicly to maintain his vigil on Arab governments and societies until real change took place, and he held to his course.

* * *

Beirut, the city where Kabbani settled after his diplomatic career, was to be a site of deep personal tragedy for the poet. He lost his second wife there in 1981, when she was an innocent victim in a bomb blast during the Lebanese Civil War. Eight years earlier, he had lost his twenty-five-year-old son, a medical student, to a heart ailment. This double tragedy left a deep mark on his life. His moving poem "Balqis," about his murdered wife, is a lengthy and powerful attack on all parties in the Lebanese Civil War who had abandoned major problems in the Arab world in order to fight each other. In "Balqis" he came close to naming those whom he believed had planted the bomb that killed his wife. Although he vowed in this poem never to write again, the prolific writer did not keep his pledge. He left Beirut after her death to reside in France and Switzerland, and finally settled in England where he lived until his death in May 1998.

There is a close harmony between Kabbani the man, his poetry, and his beliefs. This harmony produced a special musicality in his poetry that is more important than rhyme and meter. He also wrote from the heart—"I felt something, so I created something"[35]—and the qualities of innocence, truthfulness, and simplicity permeate his work. Perhaps the most important praise of any writer is the excitement and anticipation with which his or her followers wait for new work. The Arab world always anxiously awaited Kabbani's next poem, whatever the subject matter. It is still difficult to accept that there will not be one.

NOTES

1. See Salma Khadra Jayyusi, *Modern Arabic Poetry: An Anthology.* New York: Columbia University Press, 1987, p. 37.

2. See Muhyi al-Din Subhi, *Nizar Qabbani: Sha'iran wa Insanan* [Nizar Kabbani: Poet and Man]. Beirut: Dar al-Adab, 1958, p. 88.

3. See Nizar Qabbani, *Qissati Ma'a al-Shi'r* [My Story with Poetry]. Beirut: Manshurat Nizar Qabbani, 1973.

4. Ibid.

5. Nizar Qabbani, *The Complete Works*, Vol. I. Beirut: Manshurat Nizar Qabbani, 12th edition, 1983, pp. 69–71.

6. See Nizar Qabbani, *Qissati Ma'a al-Shi'r.*

7. See Subhi, *Nizar Qabbani.*

8. Ibid. The Arabic text of this letter is on p. 16.

9. Qabbani, *Qissati Ma'a al-Shi'r*, p. 100.

10. Nizar Qabbani, *Yawmiyyat Imra'a La-Mubaliya* [Diary of an Indifferent Woman]. Beirut: Manshurat Nizar Qabbani, 1968, pp. 9–10.

11. Qabbani, *Qissati Ma'a al-Shi'r*, p. 103.

12. See Muhyi al-Din Subhi, *Al-Kawn al-Shi'ri 'inda Nizar Qabbani* [The Poetic World of Nizar Kabbani]. Beirut: Dar al-Tal'a, 1977, pp. 72–74.

13. Nizar Qabbani, *The Complete Works*, Vol. II. Beirut: Manshurat Nizar Qabbani, 5th edition, 1983, pp. 87–93.

14. See Ihsan Abbas, *Ittijahat al-Shi'r al-'Arabi al-Mu'asir* [Directions of Contemporary Arabic Poetry]. Kuwait: al-Majlis al-Watani lil-Thaqafah wa al-Funun wa al-Adab, 1978, p. 176.

15. Qabbani, *The Complete Works*, Vol. I, p. 655.

16. Qabbani, *The Complete Works*, Vol. II, p. 874.

17. Nizar Qabbani, *Qassa'id Maghdoub 'alayha* [Censored Poems]. Beirut: Manshurat Nizar Qabbani, 1986, p. 16.

18. Qabbani, *The Complete Works*, Vol. I, pp. 378–384.

19. See Salma Khadra Jayyusi, *Trends and Movements in Modern Arabic Poetry*, Vol. II. Leiden: 1977.

20. Ihsan Abbas, *Ittijahat al-Shi'r al-'Arabi al-Mu'asir*, pp. 176–177.

21. These four poems are included in Qabbani, *The Complete Works*, Vol. I, pp. 334–354.

22. Munir Al-Akash, *As'ilat al-Shi'r: Fi Harakat al-Khalq wa Kamal al-Hadathah wa Mawtiha* [The Questions of Poetry: In the Movement of Creativity and the Perfection of Modernity and Its Death]. Beirut: Arab Institute for Studies and Publications, 1979. See interview with Kabbani, pp. 177–204.

23. Ibid.

24. Ibid.

25. See Ariah Loya, "Poetry as a Social Document: The Social Position of the Arab Woman as Reflected in the Poetry of Nizar Qabbani," *Muslim World* 63 (1973), p. 51.

26. Munir Al-Akash, *As'ilat al-Shi'r.*

27. Nizar Qabbani, *Hal Tasma'in Sahil Ahzani?* [Do You Hear the Neigh of My Sadness?]. Beirut: Manshurat Nizar Qabbani, 1990, Introduction.

28. Nizar Qabbani, *The Complete Works*, Vol. III. Beirut: Manshurat Nizar Qabbani, 3rd edition, 1983, p. 73.

29. Qabbani, *Hal Tasma'in Sahil Ahzani?* p. 32.

30. See Petro Martinez Montavez, *Poemas Amorosos Arabes* [Arab Love Poems]. Madrid: Istituto Hispano-Arabe de Cultura, 1975, pp. 7–41, as translated by Karl Frederick Humiston.

31. Nizar Qabbani, *Al-Shi'r Qindil Akhdar* [Poetry Is a Green Lantern]. Beirut: Manshurat Nizar Qabbani, no date, p. 21.

32. These three poems are included in Qabbani's *The Complete Works*, Vol. III, pp. 25–28.

33. Ibid., p. 13.

34. Ibid., p. 69.

35. Qabbani, *The Complete Works*, Vol. I, p. 18.

From *The Book of Love*

Oh green bird,
As long as you are my love,
God is in the sky.

ما دُمْتِ يا عُصْفُورَتِي الخَضْراءَ
حبيبتي ..
إذَنْ .. فإنَّ اللّهَ في السَّماءِ .

My lover asks me:
"What is the difference between me and the sky?"
The difference, my love,
Is that when you laugh,
I forget about the sky.

تَسأَلُني حبيبتي :
» ما الفَرقُ ما بيني وما بينَ السَّما ؟
الفَرقُ ما بيناما
أَنكِ إِنْ ضَحِكتِ يا حبيبتي
أَنسَى السَّما ...

When I fell in love,
The kingdom of the Lord changed.
Twilight slept in my coat,
And the sun rose from the west.

حِينَ أنا سَقَطْتُ في الحُبِّ
تَغيَّرتْ .. تَغيَّرتْ مملكةُ الرَّبِّ
صارَ الدُّجى ينامُ في مِعْطَفي
وتُشْرِقُ الشَّمسُ من الغَرْبِ ..

You still ask me about the day of my birth
So write down what you don't know
The day you declared your love
Is the day of my birth.

ما زلتَ تَسأَلُني عن عيد ميلادي
سَجِّل لَدَيكَ إِذَن .. ما أنتَ تَجهَلُهُ
تاريخُ حُبِّكَ لي ... تاريخُ ميلادي .

Oh, my love,
If you were at the level of my madness,
You would cast away your jewelry,
Sell all your bracelets,
And sleep in my eyes.

لو كُنتِ يا حبيبتي
بِمَسْتَوى جُنوني
رَميتِ ما عليكِ من جَواهِرٍ ..
وبِعْتِ ما لَدَيكِ من أَساوِرٍ
ونِمْتِ في عُيوني ..

All words
In the dictionaries, letters, and novels
Died.
I want to discover
A way to love you
Without words.

لأنَّ كلامَ القَوَاميسِ ماتْ
لأنَّ كلامَ المَكَاتيبِ ماتْ
لأنَّ كلامَ الروَاياتِ ماتْ
أُريدُ اكْتِشافَ طريقةِ عِشْقٍ
أُحِبُّكِ فيها .. بلا كَلِماتْ ...

I hadn't told them about you,
But they saw you bathing in my eyes.
I hadn't told them about you,
But they saw you in my written words.
The perfume of love cannot be concealed.

أنا عنكِ ما أخبرتُهم .. لكنَّهُم
رأوكِ تغتسلينَ في أحداقي ..
أنا عنكِ ما كتمتُهم .. لكنَّهُم
قرأوكِ في حبري، وفي أوراقي
للحبِّ رائحةٌ .. وليسَ بوُسْعِها
أن لا تفوحَ مزارعُ الدرّاقِ ..

I hate to love like other people.
I hate to write like other people.
I wish my mouth were a church
And my letters were bells.

أَكْرَهُ أَنْ أُحِبَّ مِثْلَ النَّاسِ
أَكْرَهُ أَنْ أَكْتُبَ مِثْلَ النَّاسِ
أَوَدُّ لو كانَ فَمِي كَنِيسَةً
وَأَحْرُفِي أَجْرَاسْ ..

Your love,
Oh you with fathomless eyes,
Is extreme,
Mystic,
Holy.
Your love, like birth and death,
Is impossible to repeat.

حُبُّكِ .. يا عَميقةَ العَينين
تَطَرُّفٌ .
تَصَوُّفٌ .
عِبادَه .
حُبُّكِ , مِثلُ الَموتِ والوِلادَه
صَعبٌ بأن يُعادَ مَرَّتين ..

From the moment you loved me
My lamp has given more light
My notebooks have blossomed
Things have changed.
I have become a child
Playing with the sun,
A prophet
When I write about you.

لماذا ؟ لماذا ؟ منذُ صِرتِ حبيبتي
يُضيءُ مَرادي ، والدَّفاترُ تُعشِبُ .
تغيَّرتِ الأشياءُ منذُ عشِقتِني
وأُصبِحتُ كالأطفالِ ، بالشَّمسِ ألعَبُ
ولستُ نبيّاً مُرسَلاً ، غيرَ أنَّني
أصيرُ نبيّاً .. عندما عنكِ أكتُبُ .

When I am in love
I make the Shah of Persia
One of my followers
I make China obey my every command
I move the seas from their customary places
And if I wanted
I could control the hands of time.

حِينَ أُكُونُ عَاشِقَاً
أَجعلُ شاةَ الفُرْسِ من رَعِيَّتي
وأُخضعُ الصّينَ لِصَوْلَجاني
وأُنقُلُ البِحارَ من مكانِها
ولو أَرَدْتُ أُوقِفُ الثَّواني .

When I am in love
I become a liquid light
And in my notebook
The poems become
Fields of mimosas and daisies.

حِينَ أَكُونُ عَاشِقاً
أُصْبِحُ ضَوْءاً سائلٌ
لا تَستَطِيعُ العينُ أَن تَرَاني
وتُصبِحُ الأشعارُ في دَفاتري
حُقُولَ ميمُوزا وأُقْوانِ .

I love you when you cry
I love your face cloudy and sad
Sadness melts us together.
I love those flowing tears
I love your face wet with tears
Women are beautiful
When they cry.

إنّي أُحِبُّكِ عندما تبكينا
وأُحِبُّ وجْهَكِ غائِماً وحزينا
الحُزْنُ يَصْهَرُنا معاً ، ويُذيبُنا
من حيثُ لا أدري ، ولا تدرينا
تلكَ الدُموعُ المطافِياتُ ، أُحِبُّط
وأُحِبُّ ، خَلْفَ سُقوطِها ، تَشْرينا
بعضُ النِّساءِ .. ووُجُوهُهُنَّ جميلةٌ
وتصيرُ أجْمَلَ .. عندما يبكينا ...

I don't know my birthday.
My face is as old as the earth,
My sadness is as old as God and the seas
My age is not important.
What is important is
My eternal love for you.

عُمْرُ وجهِي ..
مثلُ عُمْرِ الأرضِ ، آلافُ العُصُورِ
عُمْرُ حُزْنِي
مثلُ عُمْرِ اللهِ .. أو عُمْرِ البُحُورِ
يومُ ميلادي ، أنا أجهَلُهُ
فالذي يُحْسَبُ ، يا سيِّدتِي
ليسَ عُمْرِي .. إنَّما عُمْرُ شُعورِي .

32

Your eyes are like a rainy night,
My boats sink in them,
My writing disappears in their reflection,
Mirrors have no memory.

عَيْنَاكِ... مِثْلُ الليلة الماطِرَهْ
مَرَاكِبِي غَارِقَةٌ فيهِمَا .
كِتَابتِي مَنْسِيَّةٌ فيهِمَا .
إنَّ المَرَايَا مَا لَهَا ذَاكِرَهْ ..

I wrote the name of the one I loved
On the wind.
I wrote the name of the one I loved
On the water.
But the wind is a bad listener,
The water does not remember names.

كَتَبْتُ فوقَ الرّيحِ
إِسْمَ التي أُحِبُّ
كَتَبْتُ فوقَ الماءْ
لم أُدْرِ أَنَّ الرّيحَ
لا تُحْسِنُ الإِصْغاءْ .
لم أُدْرِ أَنَّ الماءْ
لا يَحْفَظُ الأسْماءْ ...

Oh traveler,
After ten years,
You are still
Like a spearhead in my side.

ما زِلْتِ يا مُسافِرَهْ
ما زِلْتِ بعدَ السَّنَةِ العاشِرَهْ
مَزْروعةً.. كالرُّمْحِ في الخاصِرَهْ ..

Our love
Has no mind or logic
Our love
Walks on water.

أرْوَعُ ما في حُبِّنا .. أنَّهُ
ليسَ لهُ عقلٌ و لا مَنْطِقٌ .
أجْمَلُ ما في حُبِّنا .. أنَّهُ
يَمْشي على الماءِ ، ولا يَغرَقُ ..

Don't worry,
My sweetest,
You are in my poetry and in my words.
You might grow old in years,
But you are ever young in my pages.

لا تَقْلَقِي .. يا حُلْوَةَ الْحُلْوَاتِ
ما دُمْتِ في شِعْرِي، وفي كَلِمَاتي
قد تَكْبُرِينَ مع السِّنينِ.. وإنَّما
لن تَكْبُرِي.. أبداً.. على صَفَحاتي.

When I travel into your eyes
I ride a magic carpet
Lifted by violet and rose clouds
Rotating like the earth
In your eyes.

وكُلَّما سَافَرْتُ في عَيْنَيْكِ ، يا حبيبتي
أُحِسُّ أنّي راكبٌ سَجَّادةً سِحْرِيَّةْ
نَعِيمَةً وردِيَّةً تَرْفَعُني ..
وبَعْدَها ، تَأتي البَنَفْسَجِيَّةْ ..
أدورُ في عَيْنَيْكِ ، يا حبيبتي
أدورُ .. مثلَ الكُرَةِ الأرْضِيَّةْ ...

Like a fish,
Quick and cowardly in love,
You killed a thousand women inside me
And became the queen.

كَمْ تُشْبِهِينَ السَّمَكَهْ
سَرِيعَةٌ في الحُبِّ .. مثلَ السَّمَكَهْ ..
جَبَانَةٌ في الحُبِّ .. مثلَ السَّمَكَهْ ..
قَتَلْتِ أَلفَ امْرَأَةٍ في داخلي
وصِرْتِ أَنتِ المَلِكَهْ ..

I am the prophet of love,
Carrying surprises to women.
Had I not washed your breasts with wine,
They would have never blossomed.
My modest miracle
Made your nipples bloom.

إِنِّي رَسُولُ الحُبِّ ..
أَحمِلُ لِلنِّساءِ مُفاجَأَتي
لو أَنِّي بِالخَمرِ لم أُغَسِّلُهُما
نَهدَاكِ .. ما كانا على قَيدِ الحَياةِ
فإذا استَدارتْ حَلَمَتَاكِ ..
فَتِلكَ أَصغَرُ مُعجِزاتي ..

Undress yourself.
For centuries
There have been no miracles.
Undress yourself,
I am mute,
And your body knows all languages.

تَعَرَّيْ .. فمنذُ زمانٍ طويلٍ
على الأرضِ لم تَسْقُطِ المُعْجِزاتْ
تَعَرَّيْ .. تَعَرَّيْ ..
أنا أَخْرَسُ
وجِسْمُكِ يعرفُ كلَّ اللُّغاتْ ...

I have changed so much.
Once I wanted you to take off everything,
To be like a naked forest of marble,
Now I want you to remain
Veiled in mystery.

كم تغيّرتُ بينَ عامٍ وعامٍ
كان هَمّي أن تَخْلَعي كُلَّ شيءٍ
وتنطلّي كغابةٍ من رَخامٍ ..
وأنا اليومَ ، لا أريدُكِ إلّا
أَنْ تكُوني إشارةَ استِفْهامٍ ..

Because my love for you
Is higher than words,
I have decided to fall silent.

لِأَنَّ حُبِّي لَكِ فَوقَ مُسْتَوَى الكَلامْ
قَرَّرْتُ أَن أَسْكُتَ ..
والسَّلامْ ...

From *One Hundred Love Letters*

أُرِيدُ أَنْ أَكْتُبَ لَكِ كَلَامًا
لَا يُشْبِهُ الْكَلَامْ.
وَأَخْتَرِعَ لُغَةً لَكِ وَحْدَكِ
أُفَصِّلُهُ عَلَى مَقَايِيسِ جَسَدِكِ
وَمَسَاحَةِ حُبِّي.

●

أُرِيدُ أَنْ أُسَافِرَ مِنْ أَوْرَاقِ الْقَامُوسْ
وَأَطْلُبَ إِجَازَةً مِنْ فَمِي.
فَلَقَدْ تَعِبْتُ مِنَ الْاِسْتِعَارَةِ فَمِي
أُرِيدُ فَمًا آخَرْ..
يَسْتَطِيعُ أَنْ يَتَحَوَّلَ مَتَى أَرَادْ
إِلَى شَجَرَةِ كَرَزْ..
أَوْ عُلْبَةِ كِبْرِيتْ..
أُرِيدُ فَمًا جَدِيدًا تَخْرُجُ مِنْهُ الْكَلِمَاتْ
كَمَا تَخْرُجُ الْحُورِيَّاتُ مِنْ زَبَدِ الْبَحْرْ
وَكَمَا تَخْرُجُ الْحِيطَانُ الْبَيْضَاءُ مِنْ قُبَّعَةِ السَّاحِرْ..

●

— I —

I want to write different words for you
To invent a language for you alone
To fit the size of your body
And the size of my love.

•

I want to travel away from the dictionary
And to leave my lips.
I am tired of my mouth
I want a different one
That can change
Into a cherry tree or a matchbox,
A mouth from which words can emerge
Like nymphs from the sea,
Like white chicks jumping from the magician's hat.

•

خُذُوا جميعَ الكُتُبِ التي قرأتُها في طُفُولتي
خُذُوا جميعَ كَرَاريسي المدرسيَّة
خُذُوا الطَّباشيرَ.. والأقلامَ.. والألواحَ السوداءَ..
وعلِّمُوني كلمةً جديدَة
أُعلِّقُها كالحَلَقِ في أُذُنِ حبيبتي..

•

أُريدُ أصابعَ أُخرَى..
لأكتُبَ بطريقةٍ أُخرَى..
فأنا أُكرهُ الأصابعَ التي لا تطولُ.. ولا تقصُر.
كما أُكرهُ الأشجارَ التي لا تموتُ.. ولا تكبُر.
أُريدُ أصابعَ جديدَةٌ..
عاليةٌ كصَواري المراكب
وطويلةٌ كأعناقِ الزُّرافاتْ
حتى أُفَصِّلَ لحبيبتي قميصاً من الشِّعرْ..
لم تلبِسْهُ قَبلي..

•

48

Take all the books
That I read in my childhood,
Take all my school notebooks,
Take the chalk,
The pens,
And the blackboards,
But teach me a new word
To hang like an earring
On my lover's ear.

•

I want new fingers
To write in another way,
High like masts of ships,
Long like a giraffe's neck
So I can tailor for my beloved
A garment of poetry.

•

أُرِيدُ أَنْ أَصْنَعَ لَكِ أَبْجَدِيَّةً

غَيْرَ كُلِّ الأَبْجَدِيَّاتْ .

فِيهَا شَيْءٌ مِنْ إِيقَاعِ المَطَرْ ..

وَشَيْءٌ مِنْ غُبَارِ القَمَرْ ..

وَشَيْءٌ مِنْ حُزْنِ الغُيُومِ الرَّمَادِيَّةْ

وَشَيْءٌ مِنْ تَوَجُّعِ أَوْرَاقِ الصَّفْصَافْ

تَحْتَ عَرَبَاتِ أَيْلُولْ .

I want to make you a unique alphabet.
In it I want
The rhythm of the rain,
The dust of the moon,
The sadness of the grey clouds,
The pain of the fallen willow leaves
Under the wheels of autumn.

فَجْأةً دخلتِ عليَّ
في صبيحةِ يومٍ من أيّامِ آذارْ
كقصيدةٍ جميلةٍ تمشي على قدَمَيْطِ ..
دخلتِ الشّمسُ معكِ ..
ودخلَ الربيعُ معكِ ..
كانَ على مكتبي أوراقٌ .. فأ وْرَقَتْ
وكان أمامي فنجانُ قهوةْ
فشربتِني قبلَ أن أشرَبهْ ..
وكان على جداري لوحةٌ زيتيّةٌ
لخيولٍ تركُضْ ..
فتركَتْني الخيولُ حينَ رأَتْكِ
وركَضَتْ نحوَكِ ..

.

52

— 2 —

That March morning when you came walking toward me
Like a beautiful poem
The sun and the spring came with you.
On my desk the papers
Turned green
In front of me a cup of coffee
Became empty before I drank it
When you appeared
The running horses
In the painting on my wall
Left me
To run to you.

•

نِزار زُرْتِني ،

في صبيحة ذلكَ اليوم من آذارْ

حَدثَتْ قشْعَريرةٌ في جَسَد الأرضْ

وسقط في مكانٍ ما .. من العالَمْ

نَيْزَكٌ مُشْتَعِلْ ..

حسِبَهُ الأطفالُ فطيرةً مَحْشُوَّةً بالعَسَلْ ..

وحسِبَتْهُ النساءْ

سِوارًا مُرَصعًا بالماسْ ..

وحسِبَهُ الرجالْ

من علامَاتِ ليلةِ القَدْرْ ...

●

54

That March morning when you visited me
The earth's body shivered,
A blazing star
Fell somewhere in the world.
Children thought the star
A honey cake.
Women thought the star
A bracelet made of diamonds.
Men thought the star
A sign from the heavens.

•

وحينَ نَزَعْتِ مِعْطَفَكِ الربيعيَّ

وجلستِ أمامي

فَراشةً تحملُ في حقائبِها ثيابَ الصيفْ

تأكَّدتُ أنَّ الأطفالَ كانوا على حَقّْ ..

و النِّساءَ كُنَّ على حَقّْ ..

والرِّجالَ كانوا على حَقّْ ..

وأنَّكِ ..

شَهِيَّةٌ كالعَسَلْ ..

وصافيةٌ كالماسْ ..

ومُدْهِلةٌ كليلةِ القَدْرْ ...

When you took off your spring coat
And sat in front of me
Like a butterfly
With a suitcase full of summer clothes,
I was certain
That all the children, women, and men
Were right.
That you were
As sweet as honey,
As pure as diamonds,
An astonishing miracle.

عندما قلتُ لكِ : « أُحِبُّكِ » ..
كنتُ أعرفُ أنني أقودُ انقلاباً على شريعةِ القبيلةْ .
وأقرعُ أجراسَ الفضيحةْ ..
كنتُ أريدُ أن أستلمَ السُّلطةْ
لأجعلَ غاباتِ العالمِ أكثرَ وَرَقاً ..
وبحارَ العالمِ أكثرَ زُرْقةً ..
وأطفالَ العالمِ أكثرَ براءةً ..
كنتُ أريدُ أن أُنهيَ عصرَ البَرْبَرِيَّةْ .
وأقتلَ آخرَ الخُلفاءْ ..
كان في نِيَّتي، عندما أحببتُكِ،
أن أُكسِّرَ أبوابَ الحريمْ ..
وأُنقذَ أثداءَ النساءِ من أسنانِ الرجالْ ..
وأجعلَ حلماتِهِنَّ ترقصُ في الهواءِ مُبتهجةً
كحبّاتِ الزَّعرورِ الأحمرْ ...

•

— 3 —

When I told you:
"I love you"
I knew
I was leading a coup
Against the tribal law,
That I was tolling the bells of scandal.
I wanted to seize power
To increase the number of leaves
In the forests.
I wanted to make the oceans bluer
And the children more innocent.
I wanted to put an end to the savage age
And to kill the last Caliph.
It was my intention
When I loved you
To break down the doors of the harem,
To protect women's breasts
From men's teeth:
So that their nipples could
Dance in the air with delight.

●

عندما قلتُ لكِ : « أُحبُّكِ » .
كنتُ أعرفُ أنِّي أخترعُ أبجديّةً جديدةً
لمدينةٍ لا تَقْرأُ ..
وأُنشِدُ أشعاري في قاعةٍ فارغةٍ
وأُقدِّمُ النبيذْ ..
لمَنْ لا يعرفونَ نعمةَ السُّكْرْ ...

‏●

عندما قلتُ لكِ : « أُحبُّكِ » .
كنتُ أعرفُ أنَّ المتوحِّشينَ سيتعقبونني
بالرماحِ المسمومةِ، وأقواسِ النَّشّابْ ..
وأنَّ صوَري سَتُلْصَقُ على كلِّ الحيطانْ
وأنَّ بصماتي سَتُوزَّعُ على كلِّ المخافرْ
وأنّ جائزةً كُبرى سَتُعْطى لمن يحملُ لهمْ رأسي
ورتَّبَ
ليُعلَّقَ على بوابةِ المدينةْ ..
كبُرتقالةٍ فلسطينيَّةْ ...

‏●

When I said:
"I love you!"
I knew
I was inventing a new alphabet
For a city that does not read,
I was reciting my poems
In an empty hall,
And I was offering wine
To those who did not know
The joys of drunkenness.

●

When I said:
"I love you"
I knew
Savages would follow me
With poison spears,
With bows and arrows.
My photograph would be plastered
On all walls.
My fingerprints
Would be distributed to all police stations,
A big reward
Would be given
To whomever carried my head to them
To be hung at the city gates
Like a Palestinian orange.

●

عندما كتبتُ اسمَكِ على دفاتر الوردْ ..
كنتُ أعرفُ ..
أنَّ كلَّ الأُميّينَ سيقفونَ ضدّي ..
وكلَّ العاطلينَ بالوراثة عن ممارسَةِ الحُبِّ .. ضدّي
وكلَّ المرْضى بورَمِ الجِنْسِ .. ضدّي ..
عندما قرّرتُ أن أقتلَ آخرَ الخلفاءْ
وأُعلنَ قيامَ دولةٍ للحُبِّ ..
تكونينَ أنتِ مليكتَها .
كنتُ أعرفُ أنَّ العصافيرَ وحدَها
ستُعلنُ الثورةَ معي ...

When I wrote your name
On the notebook of roses
I knew
All the illiterate,
All the sick and impotent men
Would stand against me.
When I decided to kill the last Caliph,
To announce
The establishment of a state of love
Crowning you as its queen,
I knew
Only the birds
Would sing of the revolution with me.

حين وزَّع اللّهُ النساءَ على الرجالْ
وأعطاني إيّاكِ ..
شعرتُ أنّه انحازَ بصورةٍ مكشوفةٍ إليَّ ..
وخالفَ كلَّ الكُتُبِ السَّماويّةِ التي أُلِّفَتِ
فأعْطَاني النبيذَ ، وأعطاهُمُ الحِنطَةْ .
أُلْبَسَني الحريرَ ، وألبَسَهُمُ القُطْنْ .
أهدى إليَّ الوردةَ ..
وأهداهُمُ الغُصْنْ ..

.

— 4 —

When God bestowed women on men
He gave you to me.
I felt
He was clearly biased toward me
And that He violated
All His heavenly books.
He gave me the wine
But gave other men the wheat,
He clothed me in silk
But clothed those men in cotton,
He gave me the rose
But gave them the thorn.

•

حينَ عرَّفني اللهُ عليكِ ..

وَذَهبَ إلى بيتهْ

فكَّرتُ أن أكتبَ له رسالةً

على وَرَقٍ أزْرَقْ ..

وأضعها في مُغلفٍ أزْرَقْ ..

وأغسلها بالدَمْعِ الأزْرَقْ ..

أبدؤُها بعبارة : يا صديقي .

كنتُ أريدُ أن أشكُرَهُ لأنَّه اختارَكِ لي ..

فاللهُ ـ كما قالوا لي ـ

لا يَسْتلمُ إلّا رَسائلَ الحُبّْ ..

ولا يُجاوبُ إلّا عليهِ ..

•

66

After God introduced you to me
He returned home.
I thought of writing Him
A letter on blue paper,
Enclosed in a blue envelope
Washed with my tears,
Calling Him,
"My dear friend,"
I wanted to thank Him
Because He chose you for me.
I wrote Him
Because I am told
God only receives
And responds
To letters of love.

•

حينَ اسْتَلَمْتُ مُكافأتي
ورجعتُ أحملُكِ على راحةِ يَدي
كزَهرةِ ماغنوليا ..
بستُ يدَ اللهْ ..
وبستُ القمرَ والكواكبْ ..
واحداً .. واحداً ..
وبستُ الجبالَ .. والأوديةَ .. وأجنحةَ الطواحينْ
بستُ الغيومَ الكبيرهْ ..
والغيومَ التي لا تزالُ تذهبُ الى المدرسةْ .
بستُ الجُزُرَ المرسومةَ على الخرائطْ ..
والجُزُرَ التي لا تزالُ بذاكرةِ الخرائطْ ..
بستُ الأمشاطَ التي سَتَتمشَّطينَ بها ..
والمرايا التي سَتَتَرَتَسمينَ عليها ..
وكلَّ الحمائمِ البيضاءْ ..
التي سَتَحملُ على أجنحتها ..
جوازَ عُمرِسكِ ..

When I received my reward
I returned home carrying you
In the palm of my hand
Like a magnolia flower.
I had kissed God's hand
And the moon and the stars
One by one.
I had kissed the mountains and the valleys,
The windmills and the clouds.
I had kissed the islands drawn on maps.
I had kissed your combs and your mirror.
I had kissed
All the white doves
That will carry
Your wedding dress
On their wings.

لم أَكُنْ يوماً مَلِكاً .

ولم أَنحَدِرْ من سُلالاتِ المُلوكْ

غيرَ أنَّ الإحساسَ بأنَّكِ لي ..

يُعطيني الشُّعورْ ..

بأنِّي أَبسُطُ سُلطَتي على القارّاتِ الخَمسْ ..

وأُسيطِرُ على نَزَواتِ المَطَرْ ..

وعَرَباتِ الرِّيحِ ..

وأَمتلِكُ آلافَ الفَنادِينِ فوقَ الشَّمسْ ..

وأَحكُمُ شُعوباً لم يَحكُمْها أحدٌ قَبلي ..

وألعبُ بكواكبِ المجموعةِ الشَّمسيَّةْ

كما يلعبُ طفلٌ بأُصدافِ البحرْ ..

لم أَكُنْ يوماً مَلِكاً ..   ولا أُريدُ أن أكونَهْ ..

غيرَ أنَّ مُجرَّدَ إحساسي بأنَّكِ تنامينَ في جَوفِ يَدي ..

يجعلُني أتوَهَّمُ ، بأنِّي قَيصَرٌ من قياصرةِ رُوسيا ..

أو أنِّي كِسرَى أنو شِروانْ ...

— 5 —

I was never a king,
I do not come from a royal family,
But the thought that you now belong to me
Gives me the feeling
Of power over five continents,
Of controlling the rain,
And the chariots of the wind,
Of possessing thousands of acres
Above the sun,
Of ruling peoples
Who have never been ruled before,
And of playing with the stars of the solar system
Like a child playing with seashells.
I was never a king
I do not want to be one;
But when I feel you sleeping
In the palm of my hand
I imagine
I'm a Russian Tsar,
A Persian Shah.

لماذا ؟

تَشْطُبِينَ كُلَّ الأزمنة ْ

وتُوقِفينَ حركةَ الحُضورْ .

وتختالِينَ في داخلي جميعَ نساءِ العشيرة ْ ؟

واحدة ً .. واحدة ْ ..

ولا أعْتَرِضْ ..

•

لماذا ؟

أُعطِيكِ ،من دونِ جميعِ النساءِ ، مفاتيحَ مُدُني

التي لم تفتَحْ أبوابَها لأيِّ طاغية ْ

ولم تَرْفعْ راياتِها البيضاءَ لأيّةِ امْرَأة ْ ..

وأطلبُ من جُنُودي

أن يَسْتقبلُوكِ بالأناشيدِ ، والمناديلِ ، وأكاليلِ الغارْ ..

وأبايِعُكِ ، أمامَ جميعِ المواطنينْ

وعلى أنغامِ الموسيقى، ورنينِ الأجراسْ

أميرة ً مَدَى الحياة ْ ..؟؟

72

— 6 —

Why do you erase history
Stop the movement of the ages
And kill within me
All other women,
One by one?

●

Why do I give you
Of all women
The keys to my cities,
Which have never opened their gates
To any tyrant,
Which have never before opened themselves
To any woman?
Why do I ask my soldiers
To receive you with songs
And laurels
And to crown you
With melodies and bells
Princess for life?

علَّمتُ أطفالَ العالَمْ
كيفَ يرسِمون اسمَكِ ..
فتحوّلتُ نَسفاهُمْ إلى أشجَار تُوتْ ..

أوصيتُ الريحَ
أَنْ تُمشّطَ خُصُلاتِ شَعرِكِ الفاحِمْ
فاعتذَرتْ بأنَّ وقتَها قصيرْ
وشَعرُكِ طويلْ ...

— 7 —

I taught the children of the world
To spell your name,
And their lips changed into cherry trees.

I asked the wind
To comb the tresses of your coal black hair
But it refused,
Saying time was short,
And your hair was long.

مَنْ أنتِ يا امرأَةْ ؟

أَيَّتُها الدَّاخلةُ كالخَنْجَرِ في تاريخي ..

أَيَّتُها الطَّيِّبةُ كعُيُونِ الأرانبْ

والناعمةُ كَوَبَرِ الخَوْخَةْ .

أَيَّتُها النقيَّةُ كأطواقِ اليا سَمِينْ .

أُخْرُجي من أوراقِ دَفاتري

أُخْرُجي من شَراشِفِ سريري ..

أُخْرُجي من فناجينِ القَهْوَةِ ..

ومَلاعقِ السُّكَّرْ ..

أُخْرُجي من أَزْرارِ قُمْصاني

وخُيوطِ مَناديلي

أُخْرُجي من كُلِّ أَشيائي الصغيرَةْ

حتَّى أستطيعَ أن أَذهبَ إلى العَمَلِ ...

— 8 —

Pure like a necklace of jasmine,
Soft as the skin of a peach,
You forced your way into my life
Like a spear.
Leave
The pages of my notebooks
The sheets of my bed,
Leave
My coffee cups
The sugar spoons,
Leave
The buttons of my shirts
The lines of my handkerchiefs,
Leave
All my little things
So I can go to work.

إنّي أُحِبُّكِ ..
ولا أَلعَبُ معكِ لُعبةَ الحُبِّ .
ولا أتخاصَمُ معكِ كالأطفالِ على أسماكِ البحرْ ..
سَمكةٌ حَمراءُ لكِ ..
وسَمكةٌ زَرقاءُ لي ..
خُذي كلَّ السَّمكِ الأحمرِ والأزرقِ ..
وظلّي حبيبتي ..
خُذي البَحرَ ، والمَراكبَ ، والمُسافرينَ ..
وظلّي حبيبتي ..
إنّي أضعُ جميعَ مُمتلكاتي أمامَكِ
ولا أفكّرُ في حسابِ الربحِ والخَسارةْ
فأنا لستُ سوى شاعرْ
كلُّ ثَروتي موجودةٌ في دفاترِي ..
وفي عَينيكِ الجميلَتينْ ..

78

I love you
But I do not play
The game of love.
I do not fight with you
Like children do
Over the fish of the sea,
A red fish for you,
A blue fish for me.
Take all the red and blue fish
But continue to be my lover.
Take the sea,
The boats,
The passengers,
But continue to be my lover.
Take all my possessions
I am only a poet
All my wealth is
In my notebooks
And in your beautiful eyes.

رمَاني حُبُّكَ على أرضِ الدَّهْشَةْ.

هَاجَمَني ، رائِحَةُ امْرَأةٍ تدخُلُ إلى مقْعَدْ ..

فاجَأني ، وأنا أُجلِسُ في المقهى مع قصيدَةْ ..

نَسيتُ القَصيدَةْ ..

فاجَأني ، وأنا أقرأُ خُطُوطَ يَدِي .

نَسيتُ يَدِي ..

داهَمَني كَديكٍ مُتَوَحِّشْ ..

فاجَأني .. وأنا قاعِدٌ على حقائِبي

أنتظِرُ قطارَ الأيَّامْ .

نَسيتُ القطارْ ..

ونَسيتُ الأيَّامْ ..

وسافرتُ معكِ إلى أرضِ الدَّهْشَةْ ..

~ 10 ~

Your love took me
To the land of wonder
Your love attacked me
Like the scent of a woman entering an elevator
Your love surprised me
While I sat in a cafe with a poem,
And made me forget the poem
Your love attacked me
Like a wild animal,
Surprising me
While I sat on the top of my suitcase
Waiting for the train of days.
I forgot the train,
I forgot the days,
While I traveled with you
To the land of wonder.

أُحِبُّكِ كالوَشْمِ على ذِرَاعٍ بَدَوِيٍّ .
وأتَسَكَّعُ معكِ على كلِّ أرصفةِ العالمْ .
ليسَ عندي جوازُ سَفَرْ ،
وليسَ عندي صُورةٌ فوتوغرافيَّةٌ
منذُ كنتُ في الثالثةِ من عُمري .

إنّني لا أُحِبُّ التصاويرْ ..
كلَّ يومٍ يتغيَّرُ لونُ عُيوني .
كلَّ يومٍ يتغيَّرُ مكانُ فمي .
كلَّ يومٍ يتغيَّرُ عددُ أسناني .
إنّني لا أُحِبُّ الجُلوسَ على كراسي المُصَوِّرينْ ..
ولا أُحِبُّ الصُّوَرَ التذكاريَّةْ ..
كلُّ أطفالِ العالمِ يتمشَّابهُونْ .
وكلُّ المُعذَّبينَ في الأرضِ يتمشَّابهُونْ
كأسنانِ المِشْطْ .
لذلكَ .. نقَعْتُ جوازَ سَفَري القديمْ
في ماءِ أحزاني .. وشربْتُهُ ..

•

82

— II —

I wear you
Like a tattoo on the arm of a Bedouin.
I wander aimlessly with you
On all the sidewalks of the world.
I have had no passport or photograph
Since I was three
I dislike pictures.
Every day the color of my eyes changes
Every day the expression of my mouth changes
Every day the number of my teeth is different
I do not like sitting
On a photographer's chair
I do not like posing for pictures.
On earth all the children and the tortured
Resemble each other
Like the teeth on a comb,
I soaked my old self
In the water of my sadness,
And drank it.

•

وقَرَّرتُ ..

أن أطوفَ العالمَ على دَرّاجة الحُرّيّةْ ..

ونَفْي الطريقةِ غيرِ الشرعيّةْ

التي تَستعمِلُطِ الريحَ عندما تُسافِرْ ..

وإذا سَأَلُوني عن عُنواني

أعْطيتُهم عنوانَ كلِّ الأرصفةْ

التي اخترتُها مكاناً دائماً لإقامَتي .

وإذا سَأَلُوني عن أوراقي

أَريتُهم عينيْكِ ، يا حبيبتي ..

فَتركوني أمُرّ ..

لأنهمْ يعرفونَ أنَّ السَّفرَ في مدائن عَينيْكِ ..

من حَقِّ جميعِ المواطنينَ في العالمْ ..

I decided
To roam the world
On the bicycle of freedom
In the same illegal way
That wind travels.
If I am asked for my address
I give
The address of all the sidewalks
That I chose as my permanent residence.
If I am asked for my papers,
I show them your eyes.
My love,
I am allowed to pass
Because they know
That traveling in the cities of your eyes
Is the right of every man.

إنتهتْ معلبُ ..

مملكةُ شُوُوني الصغيرةُ ..

لم يَعُدْ لديّ أشياءُ أُملَكِط وحدي .

لم يَعُدْ عندي زهورٌ أُنسّقُط وحدي .

لم يَعُدْ عندي كُتبٌ أقرؤُها وحدي ..

أنتِ تتدَخّلينَ بين عَيني .. وبينَ وَرَقتي ..

بينَ فمي .. وبينَ صَوتي ..

بينَ رأسي .. وبين مِخَدّتي ..

بينَ أصابعي .. وبينَ لُفَافتي ..

●

طبعاً .. أنا لا أشكُو من سُكناكِ فيَّ ..

ومن تدخّلكِ في حَركةِ يَدي ..

وحَركةِ جَفْني .. وحركةِ أفكاري ..

فأشجارُ التينِ لا تضيقُ بعصافيرها ..

والكؤوسُ لا تضيقُ بسُكْنَى النبيذِ الأحمرِ فيط ..

86

～ 12 ～

(excerpt)

My kingdom of little things
Ended with you
I no longer possess things alone,
Arrange flowers alone,
Or read books alone
You came between
My eyes and my paper,
Between my mouth and my voice,
My head and my pillow,
My fingers and my cigarette.

•

Of course
I do not complain
Of your living inside me
Or your interfering with the movement of my hands
Of the blinking of my eyes
Of the speed of my thoughts
The fig trees
Do not complain of housing too many birds
The cups do not complain
Of holding too much wine.

ليسَ لكِ زمانٌ حقيقيٌّ خارجَ كَرِفَتي .
أنا زمانُكِ .
ليسَ لكِ أبعادٌ واضحةٌ
خارجَ امتداد ذراعيَّ ..
أنا أبعادُكِ كلُّها ..
زواياكِ ، ودوائرُكِ ..
خطوطكِ المُنحنيةْ ..
وخطوطكِ المُستقيمةْ ..
يومَ دَخلتِ إلى غاباتِ صدري
دخلتِ إلى الحرِّيّةْ ..
يومَ خرجتِ منِّي
صرتِ جارِيةْ ..
واشترَاكِ شَيخُ القبيلَةْ ...

•

Out of my desire
You have no life
I am your time
You have no meaning
Beyond the reach of my arms.
I am all your dimensions,
Your corners and your circles,
Your curves and lines.
The day you entered
The forests of my chest,
You entered freedom.
The day you left,
You became a slave,
Bought by the leader of the tribe.

•

أنا علّمتُكِ أسماءَ الشَّجَرْ
وحوارَ الصَّراصير الليليَّةْ
وأعطيتُكِ عناوينَ النُّجوم البعيدةْ .
أنا أدخلتُكِ مدرسةَ الربيعْ
وعلّمتُكِ لغةَ الطيرْ
وأبجديّةَ الينابيعْ .
أنا كتبتُكِ على دفاتر المطرْ
وشراشف الثلج ، وألواح الصَّنوبَرْ
وعلّمتُكِ كيف تكمّين الأرانبَ والثعالبْ
وكيف تمشّطين صوتَ الخرزان الربيعيّةْ .
أنا أطلعتُكِ على مكاتيب العصافير التي لم تُنشَرْ .
وأعطيتُكِ خرائطَ الصيف والشتاءْ
لتغلّمي ، كيف ترتفعُ السنابلْ ،
وتُزقزقُ الصيصانُ البيضاءْ ،
وتتزوّجُ الأسماكُ بعضَها ،
ويتدفّقُ الحليبُ من ثديي القمرْ ...

•

I taught you the names of the trees
And the dialogue of the night crickets
I gave you the addresses of the distant stars.
I registered you in the school of spring
And taught you the language of the birds
The alphabet of the rivers.
I wrote your name
On the notebooks of the rain,
On the sheets of the snow,
And on the pine cones.
I taught you to talk to rabbits and foxes
To comb the spring lamb's wool.
I showed you the unpublished letters of the birds,
I gave you
The maps of summer and winter
So you could learn
How the wheat grows,
How white chicks peep,
How the fish marry,
How milk comes out of the breast of the moon

                •

لأنَّكِ ..
تَعِبْتِ من حصانِ الحرِّيةْ
فَرماكِ حصانُ الحرِّيةْ.
تَعِبْتِ من غَاباتِ صدري ..
ومن سِمفُونيَّةِ الصَّراصيرِ الليليَّةْ
تَعِبْتِ من النَّوْمِ عاريةً ..
فوق شَراشِفِ القَمَرْ ..
فتَركتِ الغَابةَ
ليأكُلَكِ الذِّئْبْ ..
ويفترَسَكِ شيخُ القبيلةْ ..

But you became tired of the horse of freedom
So the horse of freedom threw you
You became weary of the forests of my chest
Of the symphony of the night crickets
You became bored of sleeping naked
Upon the sheets of the moon,
So you left the forest
To be ravished by the leader of the tribe,
And eaten by the wolf.

السَّنَتَانِ اللَّتَانِ كُنْتِ فيها حبيبتي

هُمَا أَهَمُّ صَفْحَتَيْنِ

في كتابِ الحُبِّ المُعَاصِرْ ..

كلُّ الصَّفَحَاتِ ، قَبْلَهُما ، بيضَاءُ ..

وكلُّ الصَّفَحَاتِ ، بَعْدَهُما ، بيضَاءُ ..

إِنَّهُما خطُّ الإِسْتِواءْ

المارُّ بينَ فمي وفمكْ ..

وهُمَا المِقْيَاسُ الزَّمَنيُّ

الذي تعتمدهُ المَرَاصِدْ

وتَضْبِطُ عليه ، كلَّ سَاعاتِ العالَمْ ..

— 14 —

The two years
You were my lover
Are the two most important pages
In the book of modern love.
All the pages before and after
Were blank.
These pages
Are the lines of the equator
Passing between your lips and mine
They are the measures of time
That are used
To set the clocks of the world.

كُلَّما رأيتُكِ .. أيأسُ من قصائدي .

إنَّني لا أيأسُ من قصائدي

إلّا حينَ أكونُ مَعَكِ ..

جميلةٌ أنتِ .. إلى دَرَجةٍ أنَّني

حينَ أفكرُ بِرَوْعَتِكِ .. ألْتَبِثْ ..

تَلْتَبِثُ لُغَتي ..

وتَلْتَبِثُ مُفْرَداتي ..

خلّصيني من هذا الإرْتِكاكْ

كوني أقلَّ جَمالاً ..

حتى أستردَّ شاعرِيَّتي

كوني امرأةً عاديّةْ

تَتأكّلُ .. وتَتعطّرُ .. وتَحْبَلُ .. وتَلِدْ ..

كوني امرأةً مثلَ كلِّ النِّساءْ ..

حتى أتصالحَ مع لُغَتي ..

ومعَ فمي ..

96

When I am with you
I feel despair about writing poetry
When I think of your beauty
I gasp for breath
My language falters
And my vocabulary disappears
Save me from this dilemma
Be less beautiful
So I can regain my inspiration
Be a woman
Who uses make-up and perfume
And gives birth
Be like other women
So I can write again.

لستُ مُعلّماً ..

لأُعلّمَكِ كيف تُحبّين .

فالأسماكُ ، لا تحتاجُ إلى مُعلّمْ

لتتعلّمَ كيف تَسبَحْ ..

والعصافيرُ ، لا تحتاجُ إلى مُعلّمْ

لتتعلّمَ كيف تطيرْ ..

إسبَحي وحْدَكِ ..

وطيري وحْدَكِ ..

إنّ الحُبَّ ليس له دفاترْ

وأعظمُ عُشّاق التاريخْ

كانوا لا يعرفونَ القراءَةْ ...

— 18 —

I'm not a teacher
To show you how to love
Fish don't need a teacher
To learn how to swim
Birds don't need a teacher
To learn how to fly.
Swim and fly by yourself
Love has no notebooks,
The greatest lovers in history
Did not know how to read.

رَسائلي إليكِ ..
تتخطّاني ، وتتخطّاكِ ..
لأنَّ الضوءَ أَهمُّ من المِصْباحْ
والقصيدةَ أَهمُّ من الدفْتَرْ
والقُبلةَ أَهمُّ من الشَّفَةْ ..

رَسائلي إليكِ ..
أَهمُّ منكِ ، وأَهمُّ منّي
إنَّها الوثائقُ الوحيدةْ
التي سيَلْتَشِفُ فيها الناسُ
جمالَكِ .. وجُنُوني ..

100

— 25 —

My letters to you
Are greater and more important than both of us.
Light is more important than the lantern,
The poem more important than the notebook,
And the kiss more important than the lips.
My letters to you
Are greater and more important than both of us.
They are the only documents
Where people will discover
Your beauty
And my madness.

In the summer
I stretch out on the shore
And think of you
Had I told the sea
What I felt for you,
It would have left its shores,
Its shells,
Its fish,
And followed me.

في أيّام الصيف
أتمدَّد على رمال الشاطئ
وأُمارس هواية التفكير بكِ ..
لو أنّني أقول للبحر .. ما أشعرُ به نحوكِ
لترك شواطئَه ..
وأصْدافَه ..
وأسْماكَه ..
وتبعني ...

Every time I kiss you
After a long separation
I feel
I am putting a hurried love letter
In a red mailbox.

كلَّما قبَّلتُ ..
بعدَ طُولِ افتراقْ
أشعرُ أنَّني ،
أضعُ رسالةَ حُبٍّ مُسْتعجَلَة
في عُلْبة بريدٍ حمراءْ ...

My love runs to you
Like a white horse
Refusing the saddle and the rider
My lady,
If you knew the yearnings of horses,
You would fill my mouth
With cherries, almonds, and pistachios.

يندفعُ حبّي نحوكِ
كحصانٍ أبيضْ ..
يرفضُ سرجهُ وفارسَهْ .
لو كنتِ يا سيّدتي ؟
تعرفينَ أشواقَ الخيولْ
لملأتِ فمي
لوزاً .. وكَرَزاً .. وفُستُقاً أخضرْ ..

Every man
Who kisses you after me
Will discover above your mouth
The small grapevine
That I planted.

كلُّ رَجلٍ سَيُقبِّلُكِ بَعْدي
سَيكْتَشِفُ فوقَ فمِكْ
عَريشةً صغيرةً من الحِنَبْ
زَرَعْتُها أنا ...

Stay out of my sight
So I can distinguish between colors
Move away from my hand
So I can know the size of the universe
And discover
That the world is round.

إبْتَعِدي قليلاً عن حَدَقَتَيْ عَيْنَيَّ
حتى أُمَيِّزَ بين الألوانْ
إنْهَضي عن أصابعي الخَمْسَةْ
حتى أعرفَ حَجْمَ الكونْ ..
وأُقْنِعَ أنَّ الأرضَ كُرَوِيَّةْ ...

When rain fell on both of us
Thousands of plants
Grew on our coats.
After you left
Rain began to fall on me alone
But on my coat nothing grew.

كانَ المطرُ ينزلُ علينا معاً ..
فتنمو ألوفُ الحشائشْ
على معطفينا .
بعدَ رحيلكْ ،
صارَ المطرُ يسقطُ عليَّ وحدي
فلا ينبتُ شيءٌ على معطفي ...

— 40 —

I curl up
On the shores of your breasts
Tired
Like a child
Who has not slept
Since the day he was born.

أَ تَكَوَّمُ على رمال نَهْدَيْكِ مُتْعَبَاً
كطفلٍ لم يَنَمْ منذُ ولادتِه ..

I hope one day
You will no longer be
Fearful like a rabbit.
Then you will know
I am not your hunter
I am your lover.

آهٍ .. لو تتحرَّرِينَ يوماً
من غَريزَة الأَرانِبْ ..
وتعرفينْ ،
أنَّي لستُ صيَّادَكِ ..
لكنَّني حبيبُكِ ...

When you visit me,
Wearing a new dress,
I feel what a gardener feels
When a tree blooms in his garden.

عندما تزورينني
بثوبٍ جديدٌ ..
أشعرُ بما يشعرُ به البُستانيُّ
حينَ تُزْهِرُ لَدَيْهِ شَجَرَةٌ ..

Every time you traveled
Your perfume asked me about you
Like a child
Asking about the return of its mother.
Imagine,
Even perfume
Knows Banishment
And Exile.

كلّما سافرتِ ..
طالبَني عِطْرُكِ بكِ .
كما يُطالبُ الطفلُ بعودة أُمّهْ ..
تَصَوّري ..
حتّى العطورُ
تعرفُ الغُرْبةْ ..
وتعرفُ النّفيْ ...

هل فَكَّرْتِ يوماً .. إلى أينْ؟

المراكبُ تعرفُ إلى أينْ .

والأسماكُ تعرفُ إلى أينْ .

وأسرابُ السُّنونُو تعرفُ إلى أينْ .

إلَّا نحنُ ..

نحنُ نتخبّطُ في الماءِ .. ولا نَغْرَقْ ..

ونلبسُ ثيابَ السَّفَرِ .. ولا نُسافِرْ ..

ونكتبُ المكاتيبَ .. ولا نُرْسِلْها ..

ونحجزُ تذكرتينْ .. ..

على كلّ الطائراتِ المُسافِرَهْ

ونبقى في المَطارْ ..

أنتِ .. وأنا ..

أَجْبَنُ مُسافرينِ عَرَفَهُما العصرْ ..

~ 48 ~

Did you ever think
Of where we were going
Boats know where they are sailing,
Fish know where they are swimming,
Birds know where they are flying
Yet we flounder in the water
But do not sink
We wear traveling clothes
But do not travel
We write letters
But do not mail them
We buy tickets
On all departing planes
But stay in the airport
You and I are
The most cowardly travelers ever.

- 49 -

The day I met you
I tore up
All my maps and my prophecies
And became like an Arabian horse.
I smell the scent of your rain
Before it makes me wet,
I hear the rhythm of your voice
Before you speak
I undo your braids
Before you plait them.

مَزَّقتُ ، يومَ عرفتُكِ
كُلَّ خَرائطي ، ونُبوءاتي .
وصِرتُ كالخيُول العَربيَّةْ
أشِمُّ رائحَةَ أمطارِكْ
قبلَ أن تُبلِّلَني ..
وأسمعُ إيقاعَ صوتِكِ
قبلَ أن تتكلَّمي ..
وأفُكُّ ضَفائرَكِ بيَدي
قبلَ أن تَضفريهِ ...

Close all my books
Read the lines of my face
I look at you
With the amazement of a child
In front of a Christmas tree.

إغْلِقي جَميعَ كُتُبي
واقْرَأي خُطوطَ يَدي
أو خُطوطَ وجهي .
إنّني أتطَلَّعُ إليكِ بانْبِهارِ طفلٍ
أمامَ شَجَرة عيد الميلادْ ...

Yesterday I thought
Of my love for you.
I remembered
The drops of honey on your lips,
I licked the sugar
Off the walls of my memory.

فَكَّرْتُ أَمْسِ ، بِحُبِّي لَكِ
تَذَكَّرْتُ فَجْأَةً ..
قَطَراتِ العَسَلِ على شَفَتَيْكِ
فَلَحَسْتُ السُّكَّرَ عن جُدْرانِ ذَاكِرَتِي ..

Please,
Respect my silence,
Silence is my best weapon
Did you feel my words
When I fell silent?
Did you feel the beauty of what I said
When I said nothing?

أرجُوكِ أنْ تحترمي صَمتي
إنَّ أقوى أسْلِحَتي هُوَ الصَّمتُ .
هل شَعَرتِ ببلاغَتي عندما أسكُتُ؟
هل شَعَرتِ بِرَوْعة الأشياءِ التي أقولُها ؟
عندما لا أقُولُ شيئاً ..

لماذا تطلبينَ مِنّي أن أكتُبَ إليكِ؟

لماذا تطلبينَ مِنّي

أن أتَعرّى أمامَكِ كرجلٍ بدائيٍّ؟

الكتابةُ هي العملُ الوحيدُ الذي يُعَرّيني .

عندما أتكلّمْ ..

فإنّني أحتفظُ ببعضِ الثيابْ .

أما عندما أكتُبْ ..

فإنّني أصيرُ حُرّاً، وخفيفاً

كعُصفورٍ خُرافيٍّ لا وزنَ له ..

عندما أكتُبْ ..

أنفصِلُ عن التاريخْ ..

وعن جاذبيّةِ الأرضْ ...

وأدورُ ككوكبٍ في فضاءِ عينيكِ ..

— 55 —

Why do you ask me to write you?
Why do you ask me
To undress in front of you
Like a primitive man?
Only writing undresses me.
When I speak
I keep my clothes on,
When I write,
I become free and light
Like a weightless legendary bird.
When I write,
I separate from history
From the earth's gravity,
I turn like a planet
In the space of your eyes.

إنْزَعي الخِنْجَرَ المدفونَ في خاصِرَتي
واتْركيني أُعيشْ ..
إنْزَعي رائحَتَكِ من مَسَاماتِ جِلْدي
واتْركيني أُعيشْ ..
إمْنَحيني الفُرْصَةْ
لأتعرَّفَ على امْرأةٍ جديدَةْ ...
تشطُبُ اسْمَكِ من مُفكِّرتي
وتقطعُ خُصُلاتِ شَعْرِكِ
المُلتفَّةِ حَوْلَ عُنقي ..
إمْنَحيني الفُرْصَةْ
لأبحثَ عن طُرُقٍ لم أُمْشِ عليها مَعَكِ ..
ومقاعدَ لم أُجلسْ عليها مَعَكِ ..
وأمكنةٍ لا تذكرُكِ ذاكرَتُها .
إمْنَحيني الفُرْصَةْ
لأبحثَ عن عناوينِ النِّساءْ ..
اللَّواتي تركْتُهنَّ من أجلِكِ ..
وقتلتُهنَّ من أجلِكِ ..
فأنا أريدُ أن أُعيشْ ...

Pull out the dagger buried in my side.
Let me live.
Pull out your scent from my skin.
Let me live.
Give me a chance
To meet a new woman
To cross out your name from my diary
To cut the braids of your hair
Wrapped around my neck.
Give me a chance
To search for roads where
I have never walked with you,
For seats
Where I have never sat with you,
For places
That have no memory of you.
Give me a chance
To search for the women
Whom I left for you
And killed for you
So I can live again.

من الطائرةْ ..

يرى الإنسانُ عوالِمَهُ بِشكلٍ مُختلفْ .

يتَحرَّرُ الحبُّ من غُبارِ الأرضْ ..

من جاذبيتِها ..

من قوانينِها ..

يُصبحُ الحبُّ .. ثمرةً من القُطْنِ لا وزنَ لها .

الطائرةُ تَنزَلِقُ على سَجّادةٍ من الغَيمِ المُنتَفِخْ .

وعَيْناكِ تركُضانِ خَلفِها

كعُصفورَيْنِ فُضوليَّيْنِ

يُلاحِقانِ فَراشةً ...

•

أَحمقُ أنا ..

حينَ ظننتُ أنِّي مُسافرٌ وحدي .

فَفي كلِّ مَطارٍ نزلتُ فيهْ

عَثَروا عليكِ في حقيبةِ يَدي ..

122

~ 59 ~

(excerpt)

From the airplane
Man sees his emotions differently
Love is liberated
From the dust,
From gravity,
From laws of the earth,
And becomes a weightless ball of cotton.
The airplane glides
Over the scattered carpet of clouds,
Your eyes running behind it
Like two curious birds
Chasing a butterfly.

●

I was a fool
To think I was traveling alone.
In each airport where I landed
They found you
Inside my briefcase.

قَبْلَ أَنْ أُدْخُلَ مَدَائِنَ فَمِكِ ..
كَانَتْ شَفَتَاكِ زَهْرَتَيْ حَجَرْ
وَقَدَمَيَّ نَبِيذْ .. بِلَا نَبِيذْ ..
وَجَزِيرَتَيْنِ مُتَجَمِّدَتَيْنِ
فِي بِحَارِ الشَّمَالْ ..

— 60 —

Before I entered the cities of your mouth
Your lips were two stone flowers,
Two empty glasses of wine,
Two frozen islands in the North Seas.

قُضِيَ الأمرُ .. وأُصْبِحتِ حبيبتي
قُضِيَ الأمرُ ..
ودَخلتِ في طيّاتِ لحمي كالظُّفرِ الطويلْ ..
كاللزِّ في العُروةْ ..
كالحَلَقِ في أُذُنِ امرأةٍ إسْبانيَّةْ ..

•

كوني إِذنْ حبيبتي .. واسْلَكتي ..
ولاتُنا قِشِيني في شَرْعيَّةِ حُبِّي لكِ
لأنَّ حُبِّي لكِ شريعةْ ..
أنا أَكتُبها .. وأنا أُنفِّذُها ..
أما أنتِ ..
فمهمّتُكِ أنْ تنامي كزَهرةِ مارغريت بينَ ذراعيّ ..
وتتركيني أُحكُمْ ..
مهمّتُكِ يا حبيبتي
أن تظلَّي حبيبتي ..

～ 61 ～

(excerpt)

It is all over.
You have become my lover.
You entered my flesh like a long nail,
Like a button fitting through its hole,
Like the earrings of a Spanish woman.

•

Be my lover then
And be quiet.
Do not argue about
The legitimacy of my love for you.
My love for you is a law
I wrote.
Your task is to sleep like a daisy
Between my arms
And to let me rule.
Your task is
To remain my lover.

ماذا تقولُ أُنوثتُكِ عنّي ؟

إذا عاملتُكِ ،

كحقلٍ لا يرغبُ أحدٌ في امتلاكِه

أو كأرضٍ محايدةْ ؟

لا يدخُلُها المتحاربونْ ..

ماذا يقولُ نهداكِ عنّي ؟

إذا تركتُهما يُنثرثِران خَلْفَ ظهري ،

ونمتُ ..

ماذا تقولُ شَفتاكِ عنّي ؟

إذا تركتُهما تأكلانِ بعضَهُما

وذَهبتُ ..

~ 64 ~

(excerpt)

What would your femininity say about me
If I treated you
Like a field no one wants to own
Or like a neutral land
Where fighters never go?
What would your breasts say about me
If I slept
And left them
Whispering behind my back?
What would your lips say about me
If I departed
And left them eating one another?

عندما تكونين برفْقتي
أُحِبُّ أن أتجاوزَ جميعَ إشاراتِ المرور الحمراءْ
أُحِسُّ بشهوةٍ طفوليّةٍ
لارتكاب ملايينِ المخالفاتْ
وملايينِ الحماقاتْ ..

●

عندما تكونُ يدُكِ مَطْمورةٌ في يدي
أُحِبُّ أن أكسِرَ جميعَ ألواحِ الزُّجاجِ
التي ركّبوها حولَ الحُبِّ ..
وجميعَ البلاغاتِ الرسميّةْ
التي أصدَرَتْها الحكومةُ لمصادرة الحُبِّ ..
وأشعرُ بنشوةٍ لا حدودَ لها
حينَ تصطدمُ شظاياتُ الزُّجاجِ المكسورْ
بعَجَلاتِ سيّارتي ...

130

— 65 —

When you accompany me
I like to go through all the red lights
I feel a childish desire
To commit millions of little crimes.

•

When your hand is buried in mine
I like to break the windows
That they installed around love
To disobey official decrees
The governments issued to ban love.
I feel satisfied,
When the pieces of broken glass
Cut the tires of my car.

حينَ رَقَصْتِ معي ، في تلكَ الليلَةْ ..
حدثَ شيءٌ غريبْ .
شعرتُ أنَّ نجمةً مُتوهِّجةً
تَرَكَتْ غرفَتها في السَّماءْ
والتجأتْ إلى صَدري ..
شعرتُ كما لو أنَّ غابةً كاملةً
تَنبتُ تحتَ ثيابي ..
شعرتُ ، كما لو أنَّ طفلةً في عامِها الثالثْ
تقرأُ .. وتكتُبُ فُروضَها المدرسيَّةْ
على قُماشِ قميصي ..

●

ليسَ من عادتي أن أرقُصْ ..
ولكنَّني في تلكَ الليلَةْ
لم أكُنْ أرقُصُ فَحَسبْ
ولكنَّني .. كنتُ الرَقصْ ...

132

When you danced with me that night
Something strange happened.
I felt as if a blazing star
Left its place in the sky
And sought refuge in my chest.
I felt as if an entire forest
Was growing under my clothes.
I felt as if a three-year-old child
Was writing her schoolwork
On the fabric of my shirt.

●

It is not my habit to dance,
But that night
I was not merely dancing,
I was the dance.

يومَ تعشرينَ على رَجُلٍ ..

يقدرُ أن يحوّلَ كلَّ ذرّةٍ من ذَرّاتِكْ ..

إلى شِعرْ ..

ويجعلَ كلَّ شَعْرةٍ من شَعَراتِكِ .. قصيدَةْ

يومَ تعشرينَ على رَجُلٍ ..

يقدرُ ـ كما فعلتُ أنا ـ

أن يجعلَكِ تَغتَسِلينَ بالشِعرْ ..

وتتكحّلينَ بالشِعرْ ..

وتَتَمشّطينَ بالشِعرْ ..

فسوفَ أتوسّلُ إليكِ

أن تُسَبّحيه بلا ترّدُدْ ..

فليسَ المهِمُّ أن تكُوني لي ..

وليسَ المهِمُّ أن تكُوني لهُ ..

المهِمُّ .. أن تكُوني للشِعرْ ...

— 71 —

When you find a man
Who transforms
Every part of you
Into poetry,
Who makes each one of your hairs
Into a poem,
When you find a man,
Capable,
As I am,
Of bathing and adorning you
With poetry,
I will beg you
To follow him without hesitation,
It is not important
That you belong to me or him
But that you belong to poetry.

أعرفُ ..
ونحنُ على رصيفِ المحطَّةْ
أنَّكِ تنتظرينَ رجلاً آخَرْ ..
وأعرفُ ، وأنا أحملُ حقائبَكِ
أنَّكِ ستُسافرينَ مع رجلٍ آخَرْ ..
وأعرفُ أنَّني لم أكُنْ سوى مَروحةٍ صينيَّةٍ
خفَّفَتْ عنكِ حرارةَ الصيفْ ..
أعرفُ أيضاً ..
أنَّ رسائلَ الحُبِّ التي كتبتُها لكِ ..
لم تَكُنْ سوى مَرايا .. رأيتِ فيها غُرورَكِ ..

•

ومع هذا ..
سـأحملُ حقائبَكِ .. وحقائبَ حبيبِكِ ..
لأنَّني أستحي أن أصفعَ امرأةً ..
تحملُ في حقيبةِ يَدِها البيضاءِ
أحلى أيَّامِ حَياتي ..

136

I knew
While we were at the station
That you were waiting for another man,
I knew
While I was carrying your luggage
That you would be traveling with another man,
I knew that I was
No more than a disposable Chinese fan
Used to shield you
From the heat of the summer.
I also knew
That the love letters I wrote you
Were not more than mirrors
To reflect your pride.

●

In spite of that,
I will carry your luggage
And your lover's luggage
Because I cannot
Slap a woman
Who carries in her white handbag
The sweetest days of my life.

Your departure is not a tragedy:
I am like a willow tree
That always dies
While standing.

لَنْ يَكونَ ذِهابُكِ مَأْساوِيَّاً
كما تتصَوَّرينْ ..
فأنا كأشجارِ الصَّفْصافْ
أَموتُ دائماً
وأنا واقِفٌ على قَدَمَيَّ ...

— 81 —

While Rome burned, you burned
Do not expect me
To write an elegy for you
I am not used to
Praising dead birds.

بَعْدَما احْتَرَقَتْ رُوما .
واحْتَرَقْتِ مَعها ..
لا تَنْتَظِري مِنّي
أن أكْتُبَ فيكِ قصيدةَ رِثاءْ
فما تعَوَّدتُ ،
أن أرْثيَ العصافيرَ المَيِّتَةْ ..

هل لَدَيْكَ حَلٌّ لِقَضِيَّتِنا؟
هل لَدَيْكَ حلٌّ لِهذه السَّفينة المَثْقوبَةْ
التي لا تَستطيعُ أَن تَطفو ..
ولا تَستطيعُ أَن تَغْرَقْ ..

.

أَنا شَخْصِيَّاً ..
قابلٌ لجميعِ حُلولِكَ .
فلقد شَرِبتُ من مِلْحِ البحرِ ما فيه الكَفايَةْ ..
وشَوَتِ الشُّموسُ جِلْدِي ، بما فيه الكَفايَةْ ..
وأَكلتِ الأسْماكُ المتوَحِّشةُ من لَحمِي ..
ما فيه الكَفايَةْ ...

.

140

~ 83 ~

Do you have a solution
For our problem,
For this battered ship
That can neither float nor sink?

•

I have to accept
All your solutions
Since I have drunk enough
From the salt of the sea,
The sun has baked
Enough of my skin,
And the wild fish have eaten
Enough of my flesh.

•

أنا شخصياً ..
ضَجِرْتُ من السَّفَرْ .
وضَجِرْتُ من الضَّجَرْ .
فهل لدَيْكَ حلٌّ لهذا السَّيفْ
الذي يُخَتَرِقُنا .. ولا يقتُلُنا ؟
هل لدَيْكَ حلٌّ ؟
لهذا الأفيون الذي نتعاطاهُ .. ولا يُخَدِّرُنا ..

•

أنا شخصياً ..
أريدُ أنْ أستريحْ .
على أيِّ حَجَرٍ ، أريدُ أن أستريحْ .
على أيِّ كَتِفٍ ، أريدُ أن أستريحْ .
فلقد تعبتُ من المراكب التي لا أشْرِعَةَ لها ..
ومن الأرْصِفَة التي لا أرْصِفَةَ لها ..
فَقدِّمِي حُلُولَكِ ، يا سَيِّدَتي !
وخُذِي تَوْقيعِي عليهِ قبلَ أن أراها ..
واتْرُكِيني أنامْ ...

142

I am bored with traveling,
I am bored of being bored.
Do you have a solution
For this sword
That penetrates but does not kill?
Do you have a solution
For this opium we take
That does not make us high?

•

I want to relax
On any stone,
On any shoulder,
I am tired
Of boats without sails
Of roads without pavement.
Do offer a solution, my lady,
Which I promise to accept
So that I may sleep.

إِشْرَبي فِنْجانَ قَهْوَتِكِ ..
وَاسْتَمِعي بِهُدوءٍ الى كَلِماتي .
فَرُبَّما ..
لَنْ نَشْرَبَ القَهْوَةَ مَعاً .. مَرَّةً ثانِيَةْ .
وَلَنْ يُتاحَ لي أَنْ أَتَكَلَّمَ مَرَّةً ثانِيَةْ .

●

لَنْ أَتَحَدَّثَ عَنْكِ ..
وَلَنْ أَتَحَدَّثَ عَنّي ..
فَنَحْنُ صِفْرانِ على شِمالِ الحُبِّ ..
سَطْرانِ مَكْتوبانِ بالقَلَمِ الرَّصاصِ على هامِشِهْ .
وَلَكِنَّني سَأَتَحَدَّثُ ..
عَمّا هو أَكْبَرُ مِنْكِ .. وَأَكْبَرُ مِنّي ..
وَأَنْظَفُ مِنْكِ .. وَأَنْظَفُ مِنّي ..
سَأَتَحَدَّثُ عَنِ الحُبِّ ...

عَنْ هذه الفَراشَةِ المُدْهِشَةْ
التي حَطَّتْ على أَكْتافِنا ، وَطَرَدْناها .
عَنْ هذه السَّمَكَةِ الذَّهَبِيَّةْ ..
التي طَلَعَتْ إلينا مِنْ أَعْماقِ البَحْرْ
وَسَحَقْناها ..
عَنْ هذه النَّجْمَةِ الزَّرْقاءْ
التي مَدَّتْ إلينا يَدَها
وَرَفَضْناها ..

●

144

— 86 —

Drink your coffee,
Listen quietly to my words.
Perhaps
We will not drink coffee together again.
Perhaps I will not have the chance to speak again.

●

I will not talk about you,
I will not talk about me,
We are two zeroes on the margin of love,
Two lines written in pencil.
I will talk
About what is more transparent
Than both you and me,
I will talk
About love,
About this amazing butterfly
Lighting upon our shoulders
Only to be brushed off,
About this golden fish
Rising from the depths of the sea,
Only to be crushed,
About this blue star
Extending its hand to us
Only to be turned away.

●

ليست القضيّةُ أن تأخُذي حقيبتكِ ..
وتذهبي ..
كلُّ النساءِ يأخُذنَ حقائبهنَّ في لحظاتِ الغَضَبْ ..
ويذهبنَ ..
ليست القضيّةُ أن أُطفئَ لفافتي بعصبيّةٍ ..
في قُماشِ المقعَدْ
كلُّ الرجالِ يُحرقونَ قُماشَ المقاعدِ عندما يغضبونْ ..
القضيّةُ ليستْ بهذه البساطةْ ..
وهيَ لا تتعلّقُ بكِ .. ولا تتعلّقُ بي ..
نحنُ صِفْرانِ على شِمالِ الحُبِّ ..
وسُطْرانِ مكتوبانِ بالقلَمِ الرَّصاصِ على هامِشهْ .
القضيّةُ هي قضيّةُ هذه السَّمَكةِ الذهبيّةِ
التي رماها إلينا البحرُ ذاتَ يومْ ..
وسَحقناها بينَ أصابعِنا ..

It is not important
That you take your bag and leave,
All women take their bags and leave
Whey they are angry.
It is not the important question
That I put out my cigarettes nervously
On the upholstery of the chair,
All men do that
When they are angry.
The matter is not that simple.
It is out of our hands.
We are two zeroes in the margin of love,
Two lines written in pencil.
What is important is this:
The golden fish thrown to us by the sea
Was squashed between our fingers.

أنا مُتَّهَمٌ بالشهريارِيَّةْ
مِنْ أصدقائي .
ومِنْ أعدائي .
مُتَّهَمٌ بالشهريارِيَّةْ ..
وبأنني أجمعُ النساءْ
كما أجمعُ طوابعَ البريدْ
وعُلَبَ الكبريتِ الفارغةْ
وأُعلِّقهنَّ بالدَبابيسِ
على جُدران غُرفَتي ..
يَتَّهِمونني أيضاً بالنَرْجِسِيَّةْ ..
وبالسَادِيَّةِ .. وبالأوديبِيَّةْ ..
وبكلِّ ما في الطبِّ النفْسِيِّ من أمراضْ ..
لِيُثبِتوا أنهمْ مُثَقَّفونَ ..
وأنني مُنْحَرِفْ ...

•

87

I am accused of being like Shahrayar
By my friends
And by my enemies,
Accused of collecting women
Like stamps
Like empty matchboxes
That I pin up
On the walls of my room.
They accuse me of being narcissistic,
Sadistic,
Oedipal,
Of being disturbed
In order to prove
They are educated
And I am deviant.

●

لا أَحَدَ يا حبيبتي

يُريدُ أَنْ يستمعَ إلى إفادتي

فالقُضاةُ معقَّدونْ ..

والشهودُ مُرتشونْ ..

وقرارُ إدانَتي ، صادرٌ قبل صُدورهْ ..

لا أَحَدَ يا حبيبتي ، يفهمُ طُفولتي

فأنا أنتمي إلى مدينةٍ لا تُحِبُّ الأطفالْ ..

ولا تعترفُ بالبراءَةْ ..

ولم يسبقْ لها أنِ اشترتْ وردةً .. أو ديوانَ شعرْ ..

أنا من مدينةٍ خَشِنةِ اليَدَيْنْ ..

خَشِنةِ القلبِ .. خَشِنةِ العواطفْ ..

من كثرةِ ما ابتلعتْ من المساميرِ .. وقِطَعِ الزُّجاجِ ..

أنا من مدينةٍ جليديّةِ الأسوارْ

ماتَ جميعُ أطفالها من البَرْدْ ..

•

150

Nobody, my love,
Wants to listen to my testimony,
The judges are biased,
The witnesses are bribed,
I am pronounced guilty
Before I testify.
Nobody, my love,
Understands my childhood,
I belong to a city
That does not love children,
That does not recognize innocence,
That has never in its life
Bought a rose or a book of poetry.
I belong to a city whose hands are rough
Whose heart and emotions are hard
From having swallowed nails and pieces of glass.
I belong to a city whose walls are made of ice
Whose children have frozen to death.

●

إنَّني لا أُفكِّرُ في الاعتذارِ لأَحَدْ ..
وليس في نيَّتي أن أُوكِّلَ محامياً
يُنقذُ رأسي من حَبلِ المِشنَقةِ .
فلقد شُنِقتُ آلافَ المَرَّاتِ ..
حتى تعوَّدَتْ رقبتي على الشَّنقِ ..
وتعوَّدَ جَسَدي على رُكوبِ سيَّاراتِ الإسْعافْ ..

●

ليسَ في نيَّتي أن أعتذرَ لأَحَدْ ..
ولا أُريدُ حُكْماً بالبراءةِ من أَحَدْ ..
ولكنَّني .. أُريدُ أن أقولَ لكِ ..
لكِ وحْدَكِ يا حبيبتي ..
في جلسةٍ عَلَنيَّة
وأمامَ جميعِ الذين يُحاكمُوني
بتُهمةِ حيازةِ أكثرَ من امرأةٍ واحدةْ ..
واحْتكارِ العُطورِ .. والخواتمِ .. والأمشاطْ ..
في زَمَنِ الحربِ ..
أُريدُ أن أقولْ :
إنَّني أُحبُّكِ وحْدَكِ ..
وأتلَمَّشُ بكِ ..
كما تتَلَمَّشُ قِشرَةَ الرُّمَّانةِ بالرُّمَّانةِ ..
والدَّمعةُ بالعَينِ ..
والسِّكِّينُ بالجُرحِ ...

●

152

I am not apologizing to anyone.
It is not my intention to hire a lawyer
To save my head from the rope.
I was hanged
Thousands of times
Until my neck was used to hanging
And my body was accustomed to riding in ambulances.

●

It is not my intention to apologize.
I do not want an innocent verdict
From anyone,
But I want to tell you alone my love
In a public hearing
And in front of all those who tried me
For possessing more than one woman,
For hoarding perfumes, rings, and combs
During times of war.
I want to say:
I only love you,
And I cling to you
Like the peel clings to a pomegranate,
Like the tear clings to the eye,
Like the knife clings to the wound.

●

أُريدُ أنْ أقولْ ..

ولو لمَرَّةٍ واحِدَةْ

إنِّي لستُ تلميذاً لشَهْريارْ .

ولم أُمارسْ أبداً هوايةَ القتلِ الجَماعيّ

وتذويبِ النِّساءِ في حامضِ الكبريتْ ..

ولكنَّني شاعرٌ ..

يكتبُ بصوتٍ عالٍ ..

ويعشقُ بصوتٍ عالٍ ..

وطفلٌ أخضرُ العَيْنَيْنْ

مَشْنوقٌ على بوَّابةِ مدينةٍ

لا تعرفُ الطُّفولَةْ ..

154

I want to say
If only this one time
That I am not a disciple of Shahrayar,
I am not a murderer
And have never melted women in sulfuric acid.
Rather, I am a poet
Who writes in a loud voice,
Who loves in a loud voice.
I am a child with green eyes
Leaning on the gate of a city
That does not recognize childhood.

لماذا تُخَابِرِينَ يا سيّدتي؟

لماذا تَعْتَدِينَ عليَّ بهذه الطريقة المُتَحَضِّرَة؟

ما دامَ زَمَنُ الحَنَانِ قد مَاتْ .

وموسمُ الياسمين قد مَاتْ .

لماذا تَستعملينَ صوتَكِ

كَيْ نِغْتَالَني مرَّةً أُخرى؟

إنّني رجلٌ مّيتْ .

والمّيتُ لا يَمُوتُ مرتَّينْ ..

صوتُكِ لهُ أظافِرْ ..

ولَحْمِي ، مُطرَّزٌ كالشَّرْشَفِ الدِّمَشْقِيِّ ..

بالطَعَنَاتْ ..

●

88

Why do you telephone, my lady?
Why do you attack me in such a civilized way?
If the time for compassion is over,
And the time of jasmine is over,
Then why do you use your voice
To assassinate me again?
I am a dead man
The dead don't die twice
Your voice has nails,
And my flesh is embroidered with stabs
Like a bloody sheet.

●

التلفون .. كانَ ذاتَ يومْ
مَمدوداً بيني وبينكِ ، حَبْلٌ مِنَ الياسَمينْ
وأصبحَ الآنَ حَبْلَ مِشْنَقَةْ ..
كانَ هاتِفكِ ..
فِرَاشُ حرير ، أَسْتَلْقي عليهْ
صار صليباً من الشَّوْكِ أنزِفُ فوقَهْ .
كنتُ أفرحُ بصوتِكِ ،
عندما يَخرُجُ من سمّاعة الهاتِفْ
كعُصفور أخضَرْ ..
أ شربُ قَهوتي مَعَهْ ..
وأُدخِّنُ مَعَهْ ..
كانَ صوتُكِ جُزءاً لا يتجزأُ من حياتي
كان يَنبوعاً ، ومِظلَّةً ، ومَرْوَحَةْ ..
يحملُ لي الفَرحَ ، ورائحةَ البَراري .
صار كَنَواقيسِ يوم الجُمعة الحزينةْ
يَغسِلُني بأمطار الفَجيعةْ ..

●

158

The telephone stretched between us
Like a chain of jasmine,
Now it has become a noose.
Your telephone used to be
A bed of silk for me to lie on,
Now it is
A cross of thorns that I bleed on.
I used to be happy to hear your voice
Coming over the telephone
Like a green bird,
I used to smoke and drink my coffee with your voice.
It was essential to my life,
A spring, a parasol, and a fan
That brought me
Joy and the smell of wilderness.
Now,
Your voice sounds
Like bells on Good Friday,
Washing me with the rain of tragedy.

•

أوقفي هذه المذبحة يا سيّدتي ..

فَشَراييني كلُّها مَقطوعَةٌ ..

وأعصابي كلُّها مَقطوعَةٌ ..

رُبّما .. لا يزالُ صوتُكِ بَنَفسَجيّاً

كما كانَ من قبلُ ..

ولكنّني ـ مع الأسَفْ ـ

لا أراهُ .. لا أراهْ ..

لأنّني مُصابٌ بِعَمَى الألوانْ ..

160

Stop this torture, my lady,
My veins are blocked,
My nerves are severed.
Perhaps your voice is still violet
As it was before,
But now I can't see it
Because I'm color-blind.

تلبسينَ ملابسَ الهيبيّين
وتعلّقينَ على شعرِكِ الزُهورْ
وفي رقبتِكِ الأجْراسْ ..
تقرأينَ تعاليمَ (ماوْ)
وكلَّ كُتُبِ الثورةِ الثقافيّةْ
وتمشينَ في المَسيراتِ الطويلةْ
ترفعينَ لافتاتِ الحريَّةْ
وتطالبينَ أنْ يحكمَ الطلّابُ العالمْ
وأنْ يكسِروا جُدرانَ العالمِ القديمْ ..

•

162

You wear hippie clothes,
Hang flowers in your hair,
You wear bells around your neck
And read the sayings of Mao,
All the books of the Cultural Revolution.
You participate in long marches
Raising the banners of revolution
Demanding that the students rule the world
That the walls of the ancient world be broken.

•

وحينَ يُهاجمُكِ الحُبُّ ..

كوَحْشٍ أزرقِ الأنيابْ ..

ترتعشينَ أمامَهُ كفأرةٍ مذعُورَة

وترمينَ صورةَ (ماوُ) على الأرضْ

وترمينَ معَهُ ،

كلَّ لافتاتِ الحريَّةِ التي رفَعتْهَا

أنتِ وزميلاتُكِ ..

وتلتجئينَ باكيةً إلى صَدرِ جَدَّتِكِ ..

وتتزوَّجينَ ..

على طريقةِ جَدَّتِكِ ..

When love attacks you
Like a beast with blue fangs
You shiver
Like a terrified mouse,
You throw the picture of Mao on the floor
And the banner of revolution
That you raised,
You run crying
To your grandmother's bosom
And marry
According to your grandmother's way.

إطْمَئِنِّي يا سَيِّدَتِي !

فما جئتُ لأَشْتِمَك ،

أو لأُشْنُقَكِ على حِبال غَضَبي .

ولا جِئتُ ..

لأُراجعَ دفاتري القديمة مَعَكِ .

فأنا رَجُلٌ ..

لا يَحتَفظُ بدفاتر حُبِّهِ القديمةْ ،

ولا يعودُ إليها أبداً ..

لكنَّني جِئتُ ..

لأشكُرَكِ على زُهورِ الحُزْن التي زَرَعْتِها في داخلي

فمنكِ تعلَّمتُ أن أُحبَّ الزُّهورَ السوداءْ ..

وأَشتَريها ..

وأوزِّعُها في زَوايا غُرفَتي ..

•

— 99 —

Be assured, my lady,
I did not come to curse you
To hang you on the ropes of my anger,
I did not come to review my old notebooks with you.
I am a man
Who doesn't keep his old notebooks of love
Who never returns to his memories.
I came to thank you
For the flowers of sadness
That you planted inside me.
From you I learned
To love the black flowers,
To buy them,
To distribute them
In the corners of my room.

•

ليسَ في نيَّتي ،
أنْ أفْضَحَ انْتهازيَّتَكِ ..
أو أكْتشفَ الأوراقَ المغْشوشَةَ
التي كُنْتِ تلعبينَ بها ، طِوالَ عامَينْ ..
لكنَّني جِئْتُ لأشْكُرَكِ ..
على مَواسمِ الدَمعْ
وليالي الوَجعِ الطويلَةْ ..
وعلى كُلِّ الأوراقِ الصفراءْ
التي نَثرتِها على أرضِ حياتي .
فلولاكِ ..
لم أكْتشفْ لذَّةَ الكِتابة باللونِ الأصفَرْ ..
ولذَّةَ التفكيرِ .. باللونِ الأصفَرْ ..
ولذَّةَ العِشْقِ .. باللونِ الأصفَرْ ...

168

It is not my intention
To expose to the world your opportunist nature,
To reveal your cheating
That lasted for two years,
I came to thank you
For the seasons of tears,
For the long nights of pain,
For all the deceitful, yellow papers
You scattered
On the ground of my life.
Because of you I discovered
The pleasure of writing in yellow,
The pleasure of thinking in yellow,
The pleasure of loving with yellow.

هذه هي رِسالتي الأخيرة
ولن يكونَ بعدها رسائلْ ..
هذه .. آخرُ غَيمةٍ رماديَّةٍ
تُمطرُ عليكِ ..
ولن تعرفي بعدها المَطَرْ
هذا آخرُ النبيذ في إنائي
وبعدَهُ ..
لن يكونَ سُكْرٌ .. ولا نبيذْ ..

•

— 100 —

This is my last letter
There will be no others.
This is the last grey cloud
That will rain on you,
After this, you will never again
Know the rain.
This is the last drop of wine in my cup
There will be no more drunkenness.

●

هذه آخرُ رسائلِ الجنُونْ ..
وآخِرُ رسائلِ الطُفولةْ .
ولَنْ تعرفي بَعْدي ،
نقاءَ الطُفولةِ ، وطَرافةَ الجنُونْ ..
لقد عشِقتُكِ ،
كطفلٍ هاربٍ من المدرسةْ
يخبِّئُ في جيوبهِ العصافيرَ .. والقصائدْ ..
كنتُ مَعكِ ..
طِفْلَ الرّهلوَسةِ ، والشّرودِ ، والتناقُضاتْ ..
كنتُ طِفْلَ الشّعرِ ، والكتابةِ العصبيّةْ ..
أمّا أنتِ ..
فكنتِ امرأةً شرقيّةً الشّروشْ
تنتظرُ قدرَها ..
في خُطُوطِ فناجينِ القَهوةِ ..

●

172

This is the last letter of madness,
The last letter of childhood.
After me you will no longer know
The purity of youth
The beauty of madness.
I have loved you
Like a child running from school
Hiding birds and poems
In his pockets.
With you I was a child of
Hallucinations,
Distractions,
Contradictions,
I was a child of poetry and nervous writing.
As for you,
You were a woman of Eastern ways
Waiting for her fate to appear
In the lines of the coffee cups.

•

ما أتعسَكِ يا سيّدتي!
فلَنْ تكوني في الكُتبِ الزَّرقاءِ .. بعدَ اليومْ
ولن تكوني في وَرَقِ الرسائلْ ،
وبكاءِ الشُّموعْ ..
وحَقيبةِ مُوزِّعِ البريدْ .
لَنْ تكوني في عرائسِ السُّكَّرْ
وطيّاراتِ الوَرقِ الملوّنةْ
لَنْ تكوني في وَجَعِ الحُروفْ
أو في وَجَعِ القصائدْ ..
فلقد نفَيتِ نفسَكِ خارجَ حدائقِ طفولتي
وأصبحتِ نثراً ..

174

How miserable you are, my lady,
After today
You won't be in the blue notebooks,
In the pages of the letters,
In the cry of the candles,
In the mailman's bag.
You won't be
Inside the children's sweets
In the colored kites.
You won't be in the pain of the letters
In the pain of the poems.
You have exiled yourself
From the gardens of my childhood
You are no longer poetry.

Other Poems

في الحبّ البحريّ

أنا بحرُكِ ، يا سيّدتي
فلا تسأليني عن تفاصيل الرحلةْ
ووقتِ الإقلاعِ والوصولْ .
كلُّ ما هو مطلوبٌ منكِ
أن تنسَيْ غرائزَكِ البرّيّةْ
وتُطيعي قوانينَ البحرْ ..
وتخترقيني كسمكةٍ مجنونةْ
تَشطُرُ السفينةَ إلى نصفَيْنْ ..
والدُّفَّةَ إلى نصفَيْنْ ..
وحياتي إلى نصفَيْنْ ..

About Sea Love

I am your sea,
Do not ask me
About the upcoming voyage.
All you need to do is
Forget your earthly instincts
Obey the law of the sea
Penetrate me like a mad fish,
Split the ship,
The horizon,
My life
Into pieces.

أقرأ جَسَدَكِ .. وأتثَقَّفْ

يومَ طَرَدوني من القبيلةْ
لأني تركتُ قصيدةً على باب خَيْمَتِكِ
وتركتُ لكِ محبرطا .. وردةً ..
بدأتْ عصورُ الإنحطاطْ .
إنّ عُصورَ الإنحطاطِ ليستِ الجَهْلَ
بمبادئ النّحو والصّرفْ ..
وكلّنّظَّطُ الجَهْلَ بمبادئ الأُنوثةْ
وشطْبُ أسماءِ جميعِ النّساءِ
من ذاكرة الوَطَنْ ...

•

I Learn by Reading Your Body

When I was expelled from the tribe
For leaving a poem and a rose
At the door of your tent,
The age of decay began,
An age familiar with grammar and syntax
But ignorant about femininity,
An age guilty of
Erasing all women's names
From the nation's memory.

•

آهِ .. يا حبيبتي .

ما هو هذا الوطنُ الذي يتعاملُ مع الحُبِّ

كرجُلِ بوليسْ ؟

فيعتبرُ الوردةَ مؤامرةً على النظامْ

ويعتبرُ القصيدةَ منشوراً سرّياً ضدّه .

ما هو هذا الوطنْ ؟

المَرْسومُ على شكلِ جَرادةٍ صَفْراءَ ..

تزحَفُ على بطنِظ من المحيطِ إلى الخليجْ .

من الخليجِ الى المُحيطْ .

والذي يَتكلّمُ في المنظرِ كقدّيسِّ

ويَدُوخُ في الليل على سُرّةِ امْرأةْ ...

•

Oh my love,
What kind of a nation is this?
Dealing with love like a policeman
Considering the rose
A conspiracy against the system
Considering the poem
A secretive leaflet.
What kind of a nation is this?
Taking the shape of a yellow locust
Crawling on its belly
From the ocean to the Gulf
From the Gulf to the ocean,
Speaking like a saint in the daytime
Getting drunk over a woman's navel at night.

●

ما هو هذا الوطنْ ؟
الذي أَلْغَى مادَّةَ الحُبِّ من مَناهجِه المدرسيَّةْ.
وألغى فنَّ الشِّعرْ ..
وعُيونَ النِّساءْ ..
ما هو هذا الوطنْ ؟
الذي يُمارسُ العُدوانَ على كُلِّ غَمامةٍ ماطِرةْ
ويفتحُ لكلِّ نَهرٍ .. ملفًّا سِرِّيًّا
ويُنظِّمُ مع كلِّ وردةٍ ..
مَحْضَرَ تحقيقْ ..

•

184

What kind of a nation is this?
Deleting love from its curriculum
The art of poetry,
The mystery of women's eyes.
What kind of a nation is this?
Battling each rain cloud,
Opening a secret file for each breast,
Filing a police report for every rose.

•

أيّتها المدهشة كألعاب الأطفالْ
إنّني أعتبرُ نفسي متحضّراً ..
لأنّي أحبّكِ ..
كلُّ زمنٍ قبلَ عينيكِ هو احتمالْ .
وكلُّ زمنٍ بعدَهُما ، هو شظايا .
فلا تسأليني لماذا أنا مَعكِ ..
إنّني أريدُ أن أخرجَ من تخلّفي ..
وأدخُلَ في زَمَن الماءْ ..
أريدُ أن أخرجَ من بُداوتي
وأجلسَ تحتَ الشجرْ .
وأغتسلَ بماء الينابيعْ
وأتعلّمَ أسماءَ الأزهارْ ..

•

186

You amaze me
Like a child's toy
I feel civilized because I love you
Before you, time did not exist
After you, it split into pieces
Do not ask me why I'm with you
I want to be rid of my backwardness
Escape my Bedouin ways.
I want to sit beneath a tree,
Bathe in spring water,
Learn the names of the flowers.

●

أُرِيدُ أَنْ تُعَلِّمِينِي القِرَاءةَ والكِتَابَةْ ..
فالكِتَابةُ على جَسَدِكِ ، أَوَّلُ المعرِفَةْ ،
والدُّخُولُ إليهِ دُخُولٌ إلى الحَضَارَةْ ..
ومَنْ لا يقرأُ دَفاتِرَ جَسَدِكِ ..
يبقى طُولَ حياتِهِ أُمِّياً ...

I want you to teach me the first knowledge
Of reading and writing on your body
Whoever does not read
The notebooks of your body
Will remain illiterate
All his life.

إلى حبيبتي في رأس السنة

إنَّني أُحبُّكِ ..
ولا أُريدُ أن أربطَكِ بالماءِ، أو بالريحِ
ولا بحَركاتِ المَدِّ والجَزرْ .
أو ساعاتِ الخُسوفِ والكُسوفْ
لا يعنيني ما تقولُه المراصدْ
وخُطوطُ كفِّ جبينِ القهوةْ ..
فعيناكِ وحدَهُما هُما النبوءةْ ...

To My Love on New Year's Eve

I love you
And I don't want
To link you
To the water or the wind,
To the ebb and flow of the sea,
To the hours of the solar eclipse
I don't care
About what the astronomers say
About what appears
In the lines of the coffee cups.
Your eyes are
The only prophecy.

هل تسمحين لي أن أُصطاف؟

أيتها المرأةُ التي تستوطنُ جهازي العصبيَّ .
هل تسمحينَ لي أن أُصطافَ كما يصطافُ الآخرونْ ؟
وأتمتعَ بأيام الجَبلِ .. كما يتمتعُ الآخرونْ .
الجبلُ مَرْوَحةُ حريرٍ إسبانيةٌ ..
وأنتِ مرسومةٌ عليهِ ..
وعصافيرُ عَينيكِ ..
تأتي أفواجاً أفواجاً من جهةِ البحرْ ..
كما تطيرُ الكلماتُ من أوراقِ دفترٍ أزرقْ .
هل تسمحينَ لذاكرتي أن تكسرَ حصارَ رائحتِكْ ؟
وتنشمَّ رائحةَ الحَبَقِ ، والزَّعْتَر البريّ ..
هل تسمحينَ لي .. أن أجلسَ على الشُّرْفةِ الصيفيّةْ ؟
دونَ أن يتسلّقَ صوتُكِ .. كعريشةٍ زرقاءْ
على نافذة بيتي ؟.

Will You Allow Me to Take a Holiday?

Woman who dwells inside me
Will you allow me
To take a holiday
And enjoy days in the mountains
As others do?
The mountain is
A silk Spanish fan
You are painted on it
The birds of your eyes
Come in flocks
From the seaside
Like words
Flying out of the pages
Of a blue notebook.
Will you allow my memory
To break through
The blockage of your scent
To smell
The basil and the wild thyme?
Will you allow me
To sit on the summer balcony
Without your voice
Climbing to me?

تأخذينَ في حقائبكِ الوقتَ ، وتُسافرينْ

تجوّلتُ في شوارع وجهِكِ
أيّتُها المرأةُ التي كانتْ في سالف الزَّمان حبيبتي ..
سألتُ عن فندقي القديمْ .
وعن الكُشكِ الذي كنتُ أشتري منه جرائدي .
وأوراقَ اليانصيب التي لا تربَحْ ..
لم أجدِ الفُندقَ ، ولا الكُشكْ ..
وعلمتُ أن الجرائدْ ..
توقَّفتْ عن الصُّدور بعد رحيلِكِ .
كانَ واضحاً أنّ المدينةَ قد انتقلتْ ..
والأرصفةَ قد انتقلتْ ..
والشمسَ قد غيّرتْ رقم صندوقِها البريديّ .
والنّجومَ التي كُنّا نستأجِرُها في مَوسم الصيفْ
أصبحتْ بَرسم التسليمْ ..
كانَ واضحاً ، أنّ الأشجارَ غيّرتْ عناوينَها ..
والعصافيرَ أخذَتْ أولادَها ..
ومجموعةَ الأُسطوانات الكلاسيكيّة التي تحتفظ بِها ..
وهاجَرتْ ..
والبحرَ رَمى نفسَهُ في البحرِ ..
وماتْ ...

•

194

Time Travels with You When You Leave

I walked through
The streets of your face
Oh woman who used to be my lover.
I asked about my old hotel,
About the stand
Where I bought my newspaper,
The lottery tickets
That never won.
I found neither the hotel,
Nor the stand.
I learned
That the newspapers were no longer printed
After your departure,
That the city and the sidewalk
Had moved,
That the sun had changed its address,
And that the stars
We rented during the summer
Had been sold.
The trees had changed their locations,
The birds had migrated
With their young and their music.
The sea had thrown itself
Upon its own waves
And died.

•

توقَّفي عن النُّموِّ في داخلي ..
أيَّتُها المرأةُ التي تَتَنَاسَلُ تحتَ جِلْدي كغَابَةٍ ..
ساعِديني .. على كَسْرِ العاداتِ الصغيرةِ التي كوَّنتِها معي ..
وعلى اقتلاعِ رائحتِكِ ..
من قُماشِ السَّتائرِ .. ورُفوفِ الكُتُبِ .. وبلَّورِ المَزْهرِيَّاتْ ..
ساعِديني على تَذكُّرِ اسْمي ..
الذي كانُوا يُنادُونني به في المدرسَةْ ..
ساعِديني .. على تذكُّرِ أشكالِ قصائُدي
قبلَ أن تأخُذَ شكلَ جَسَدِكْ ..
ساعِديني .. على استعادةِ لُغتي
التي فَصَّلتُ مُفرَداتِها عليكِ ..
ولم تعُدْ صالحةً لسواكِ من النِّسَاءْ ..

                    •

تَجوَّلتُ في أزقَّةِ صوتِكِ المُمطِرةْ
بحثاً عن مِظلَّةٍ تقيني من الماءْ .
كانَ في يدي خريطةُ المدينةِ التي أحببتُكِ فيها ..
وأسماءُ الأندية اللّيليَّةِ التي راقصتُكِ فيها ..
ولكنَّ شُرطيَّ السيرِ ، سَخِرَ من بلاهتي
وأخبَرَني أنَّ المدينةَ التي أبحثُ عنها
قد ابتلعَها البحرُ ..
في القرنِ العاشرِ قبلَ الميلادْ ..

                    196

Oh woman who roots in my skin like a forest,
Stop growing inside me
Help me
To break the little habits
We developed together,
To extricate your scent
From the draperies,
The bookshelves,
The crystal vases.
Help me
To remember the name
I was called in school.
Help me
To remember the form of my poems
Before they take the shape of your body.
Help me
To regain my language
Which cannot be spoken
To any other woman but you.

                    •

I wandered
In the rainy alleys of your voice
In search of an umbrella.
I carried the map of the city
Where I loved you,
The names of the nightclubs
Where I danced with you,
But the policemen mocked me
And told me
That the city I was searching for
Had been swallowed by the sea
In the tenth century.

الحبُّ في الإقامة الجبريَّة

أَستأذنُكِ بالإنصرافْ ..
فالدمُ الذي كنتُ أَحسبُ أَنه لا يُصبح ماءً
أَصبحَ ماءً .
والسماءُ التي كنتُ أَعتقدُ أَن زُجاجها الأزرقْ
غيرُ قابلٍ للكَسرِ .. إنكسَرتْ .
والشمسُ .. التي كنتُ أَعلّقها كالخَلق الإسبانيّ
في أُذنيكِ ..
وَقعتْ منّي على الأرضِ وتهشّمتْ ..
والكلماتُ التي كنتُ أُغطّيكِ بها عندما تنامينْ ..
هربَتْ كالعصافيرِ الخائفةْ ..
وترَكتُكِ عاريةْ .. ..

●

198

Love During House Arrest

I ask for your permission to leave
Since blood
Which cannot be changed into water
Has changed into water.
The sky
Whose blue glass
I believed to be unbreakable
Has broken.
The sun
Which I hung on your ear
Like a Spanish earring
Has fallen on the ground
And shattered.
The words
That I used to cover you
While you slept
Have fled like terrified birds
Leaving you naked.

●

أَستأذنُكِ بالتَّرَدُّجِ من هذا المطبِّ الروائيِّ
بين نهديْكِ ..
فلم تَعُدْ عندي شهوةٌ لِمَا قميصيْكِ ..
أو لِمَضاجعتيْكِ ..
لم أَعُدْ متحمِّساً للهجومِ على أيِّ شيءٍ ..
أو للدفاع عن أيِّ شيءٍ .
فقد سقَطْنا في الزَّمَنِ الدائريِّ
حيثُ المسافةُ بين يَدي وخاصرتِكِ ..
لا تتغيَّرْ ..
وبينَ أَنفي.. ومَسامات جِلدِكِ ..
لا تتغيَّرْ ..
وبينَ زَنزَانة فَخذيْكِ.. وساحةِ إعدامي ..
لا تتغيَّرْ ...

•

200

I ask for your permission to leave
This turbulence between your breasts
I no longer have
The desire to talk to you
To make love to you
I am no longer enthusiastic
About attacking anything
Or defending anything
We have fallen into circular time
Where the distance
Between my hand
And your waist
Does not change,
The distance
Between my sense of smell
And the scent of your body
Does not change,
The distance
Between your thighs
And the circle of my death
Does not change.

●

أَسْتَأْذِنُكِ ، بِالخُرُوجِ مِنْ هَذَا الزَّمَنِ الضَّيِّقْ ..
زَمَنِ الجِنْسِ المُعَلَّبْ ..
وَالعَوَاطِفِ الجَاهِزَةِ كَأَفْطَارِ الصَّبَاحْ
وَالقُبَلَاتِ الَّتِي أُسَدِّدُهَا مُرْغَماً
كَكِمْبِيالَةٍ مُسْتَحَقَّةِ الدَّفْعْ ...

●

أَسْتَأْذِنُكِ .. بِأَخْذِ إِجَازَةٍ طَوِيلَةْ ..
فَلَقَدْ تَعِبْتُ مِنْ حَالَةِ العِشْقْ ..
وَالحُبِّ .. الَّتِي أَنَا فِيطْ .
وَتَعِبْتُ مِنْ هَذِهِ الشِّقَّةِ المَفْرُوشَةْ
الَّتِي صَارَتْ عَوَاطِفِي ، مُرَبَّعَةً كَجُدْرَانِطْ
وَشُرُوقِي مُسْتَطِيلَةً كَدَهَالِيزِهَا..
وَطُمُوحِي وَالحُمَّا كَسَقْفِطْ ..

●

202

I ask for your permission to leave
This narrow time
Of canned sex,
Instant emotions,
Kisses
That I pay in spite of myself
Like an overdue bill.

●

I ask for your permission to leave,
To take a long vacation
I am tired of feeling
No love and no longing.
I am tired of this furnished apartment
Where my emotions are square
Like its walls
My lust is
As long as its hallways
My ambitions are
As low as its ceilings.

●

أُرِيدُ أَنْ أُطْلِقَ الرَّصَاصْ

عَلَى مَلاَبِسِكِ المَسْرَحِيَّةْ ..

وعَلى عُدَّةِ الشُّغْلِ التي تَسْتَعْمِلِينَهَا فِي التَّشْخِيصْ

عَلى الأَخْضَرِ ، واللِّيلَكِيِّ ،

عَلى الأَزْرَقِ ، والبُرْتُقَالِيِّ ..

عَلى عَشَراتِ القَوَارِيرِ التي جَمَعْتِ فيها فِضَائِلَ دَمِي ...

عَلى غَابَةِ الخَوَاتِمِ والأَسَاوِرْ ..

التي اسْتَعْمَلْتِها لابْتِزَازِي .

عَلى الأَحْزِمَةِ الجِلْدِيَّةِ العَريضَةْ

التي اسْتَعْمَلْتِها فِي جَلْدِي

عَلى دَبابِيسِ الشَّعرْ ..

ومَبَارِدِ الأَظَافِرْ ..

والسَّلاَسِلِ المَعْدِنِيَّةْ ..

التي لجَأْتِ إِلَيْها، لأَخْذِ اعْتِرافاتِي ...

•

I want to rip up
Your theatrical clothes
Shoot at
Your tools and your masks.
I want to break
The dozens of colored bottles
You filled with my blood,
I want to chop down
The forests of rings and bracelets
You used to blackmail me.
I want to rip up
The wide leather belts
You whipped me with.
I want to destroy
The hairpins,
Nail files,
And metal chains
That you used to make me confess.

●

أُريدُ أَنْ أُطْلِقَ الرَّصاصَ
على كُلِّ قَصائِدي التي كَتَبْتُها لكِ ..
وعلى كُلِّ الإِهْداءَاتِ الهِيسْتِيرِيَّةِ
التي صَدَرَتْ عنّي ,
في ساعاتِ الحُبِّ الشَّديدِ ..
أَوْ ..
في ساعاتِ الغَباءِ الشَّديدِ ..

206

I want to shoot
At all the poems I wrote you
At all the hysterical dedications
That I issued
In moments of intense love
Or
In moments of intense stupidity.

إنَّ الأُنوثةَ من عِلْمِ ربّي

يَذُوبُ الحَنانُ بِعَيْنَيْكِ مِثلَ دَوَائِرِ مَاءٍ ..
يذوبُ الزمانُ ، المكانُ ، الحقولُ ، الموتُ ،
الحِجارُ ، المراكِبُ ..
يَسقُطُ وجهي على الأرضِ مِثلَ الإناءْ
وأحمِلُ وجهي المُكَسَّرَ بين يَدَيَّ ..
وأحلُمُ بامْرَأَةٍ تشتريهِ ..
ولكنَّ من يشترونَ الأواني القديمةَ
قد أخْبَرُوني :
بأنَّ الوُجوهَ الحزينةَ لا تَشْتَريطِ النِّساءْ ..

•

208

Women, The Knowledge of God

Tenderness fades in your eyes
Like circles of water.
Time, space, fields,
Houses, seas, ships
Disappear.
My face falls to the ground like a broken vase
That I carry in my hands,
Dreaming of a woman who will buy it,
But I am told
That women do not buy sad faces.

●

وَصَلْنا إلى نُقْطَةِ الصِّفْرِ ..

ماذا أَقولُ؟ وماذا تَقولِينَ؟

كلُّ المَواضيعِ صارَتْ سَواءْ ..

وصار الوَراءُ أَماماً ..

وصار الأمامُ وَراءْ ..

وصلْنا الى ذَرْوَةِ اليأسِ ..

حيثُ السَّماءُ رَصاصْ ..

وحيثُ العِناقُ قِصاصْ ..

وحيثُ مُمارَسةُ الجِنسِ .. أقْسى جَزاءْ ..

•

We reached the point
Where we did not know what to say
All subjects became the same
The foreground merged with the background.
We reached the peak of despair
Where the sky was a bullet,
Embracing was retaliation,
Making love was the severest punishment.

•

تُحبّينَ .. أو لا تُحبّينَ ..

إنَّ القضيّةَ تَعنيكِ أنتِ ، على أيّ حالٍ .

فلستُ أُجيدُ القراءةَ في شَفتيْكِ ..

لكيْ أتنبّأَ في أيّ وقتٍ ..

سينفجرُ الماءُ تحت الرمالْ .

وفي أيّ شهرٍ تكونينَ أكثرَ عُشْباً ..

وأكثرَ خِصْباً ..

وفي أيّ يومٍ تكونينَ قابلةً للوصالْ ..

It is up to you to love me.
I do not know how to read your lips
To predict when
Water will explode beneath the sands,
I do not know
During which month
You will be more abundant
And fertile
Or on which day
You will be ready for
The communion of love.

سأقولُ لكِ أُحبُّكِ

سأقولُ لكِ : أُحبُّكِ .
حين تنتهي كلُّ لغاتِ العِشْقِ القديمةْ .
فلا يبقى للعُشّاقِ شيءٌ يقولونَهُ ، أو يفعلونَهْ .
عندئذٍ ستبدأُ مُهمّتي في تغييرِ حجارةِ العالمْ ..

•

سأقولُ لكِ : أُحبُّكِ .
عندما أشعرُ أنَّ كلّما فيكِ صارتْ تستحقُّكِ ..
وتضيقُ المسافةُ بين عينيْكِ وبين دفاتري .
سأقولُها ، عندما أُصبِحُ قادراً ، على اسْتِحضارِ طفولتي
وخُيولي ، وعسَاكري ، ومراكبي الوَرقيّةْ ..
واستِعادةِ الزَّمنِ الأزرقِ معلّبٍ ، على شاطئٍ بيروتْ ..
حين كُنتِ ترتعشينَ كَسَمكةٍ بين أصابعي ..
فأُغطّيكِ حين تنامينْ ..
بشرْشَفٍ من نُجومِ الصيفْ ..

•

214

I Will Tell You: I Love You

I will tell you: I love you
When all old love languages die
And nothing remains for lovers to say or do
Then my task
To move the stones of this world
Will begin.

●

I will tell you: I love you
When I feel
That my words are worthy of you
And the distance between your eyes
And my notebooks disappears,
I will say it when I am able
To evoke my childhood,
My horses, my troops
And my cardboard boats
And able to regain
The blue time with you
Upon Beirut's shores
When you were tired,
Shivering like a fish between my fingers,
And I covered you
With a sheet made of summer stars.

●

سأقولُ لكِ « أُحِبُّكِ » ..

عندما أبرأُ من حالة الفِصَام التي تُمَزِّقني ..

وأعودُ شخصاً واحداً .

سأقولها ، عندما تتصالحُ المدينةُ والصحراءُ في داخلي .

وترحلُ كلُّ القبائلِ عن شواطئِ دمي .

وأتحَرَّرُ من الوشمِ الأزرقِ المحفورِ على جسدي ..

ومن كلِّ وصفاتِ الطِّبِّ العربيِّ

التي جرَّبتُها على مدى ثلاثينَ عاماً

فشوَّهتْ دُكّورَفي ..

وأصدرتْ حُكْماً بجلدِكِ ثمانينَ جَلْدَةً ..

بتُهْمَةِ الأُنوثَةْ ..

لذلكَ.. لن أقولُ لكِ أُحِبُّكِ ..

فالأرضُ تأخذُ تسعةَ شهورٍ لتُطلِعَ زهرةً ..

والليلُ يتعذّبُ كثيراً ، ليلِدَ نجمةً ..

والبشريَّةُ تنتظرُ ألوفَ السنواتِ ، لتُطلِعَ نبيّاً ..

فلماذا لا تنتظرينَ بعضَ الوقتِ ..

لتُصبِحي حبيبتي ؟؟

216

I will tell you: I love you
When I am cured of my schizophrenia
And become a single person.
I will say it
When the city and the desert inside me
Are reconciled,
When all the tribes leave my blood,
When I will be free of the blue tattoo
Engraved on my body,
Free of old Arab remedies
Which I tried for thirty years
And which told me
To lash you eighty times
For being a woman.
Perhaps I will not say:
I love you.
It takes nine months
For a flower to bloom,
The night suffers a great deal
In giving birth to a star,
Humanity waits one thousand years
To produce a prophet,
Why don't you wait then
To be my lover.

The Talk of Her Hands

Keep silent,
The most beautiful voice
Is the talk of your hands
On the table.

حَديثُ يَدَيْطِ

قليلٌ من الصَّمتِ ..
يا جَاهِلَة .
فأَجملُ من كلِّ هذا الحَديثْ
حَديثُ يَدَيْكِ
على الطَّاوِلَةْ ...

I Am Afraid

I am afraid
To express my love to you
Wine loses its fragrance
When poured into a goblet.

أُخافُ

أُخَافُ أَنْ أَقُولَ للتي أُحِبُّ
» أُحِبُّكِ «.
فَالخَمْرُ في جِرَارِها
تَخْسَرُ شيئاً ، عندما نَصُبُّها ...

مَنْ مِنْكُمَا أَحْلَى؟

شِعْرِي .. وَوَجْهُكِ .. قِطْعَتَا ذَهَبٍ
وَحَمَامَتَانِ ..   وَزَهْرَتَا دِفْلَى .
مَا زِلْتُ مُحْتَاراً   أَمَامَكُمَا .
مِنْ مِنْكُمَا؟ مَنْ مِنْكُمَا؟   أَحْلَى ..

⤙ Who Is the Prettiest? ⤙

My poetry and your face
Are two pieces of gold,
Two doves and two oleander flowers
I am still confused
Who is the prettiest?

أغتصبُ العالَمَ بالكلماتْ

أغتصبُ العالَمَ بالكلماتْ .
أغتصبُ اللغةَ الأُمَّ .. النحوَ .. الصرفَ ..
الأفعالَ .. الأسماءْ ..
أجتاحُ بطاراتِ الأشياءْ
وأُشكّلُ لغةً أُخرى
فيطِلُ سرُّ النارِ ، وسرُّ الماءْ .
وأُضيئُ الزمنَ الآتي ..
أوقِفُ في عينيكِ الوقتَ ..
وأمحو الخطَّ الفاصلَ بينَ اللحظةِ والسنواتْ ..

222

I Conquer the Universe with Words

I conquer the universe with words.
I ravish the mother tongue,
The syntax, the grammar,
The verbs, and the nouns,
I violate the virginity of things
And form another language
That conceals the secret of fire
And the secret of water.
I illuminate the coming age
And stop the time in your eyes,
Erasing the line that separates
This moment from the years.

About the Book

～

NIZAR KABBANI'S POETRY HAS BEEN DESCRIBED AS "MORE POWERFUL than all the Arab regimes put together" *(Lebanese Daily Star)*. *Arabian Love Poems* is the first English-language collection of his work. Frangieh and Brown's elegant translations are accompanied by the striking Arabic texts of the poems, penned by Kabbani especially for this collection.

Kabbani was a poet of great simplicity—direct, spontaneous, musical, using the language of everyday life. He was a ceaseless campaigner for women's rights, and his verses praise the beauty of the female body, and of love. He was an Arab nationalist, yet he criticized Arab dictators and the lack of freedom in the Arab world. He was the poet of Damascus: "I am the Damascene. If you dissect my body, grapes and apples will come out of it. If you open my veins with your knife, you will hear in my blood the voices of those who have departed."

NIZAR KABBANI was born in Syria in 1923, to a traditional, well-to-do family. He served in Syria's diplomatic corp for more than 20 years (1945-1966), but settled for political reasons in London. He died on April 30, 1998; at his request, he was buried in Damascus.

BASSAM K. FRANGIEH is professor of Arabic at Yale University. CLEMENTINA R. BROWN translates and interprets from Arabic, French, and Spanish into English.